Vivienne Beisel

"Do not take them from myself and my children forever"

Vivienne Beisel

"Do not take them from myself and my children forever"

Aboriginal Water Rights in Treaty 7 Territories and the Duty to Consult

VDM Verlag Dr. Müller

Impressum/Imprint (nur für Deutschland/ only for Germany)
Bibliografische Information der Deutschen Nationalbibliothek: Die Deutsche Nationalbibliothek verzeichnet diese Publikation in der Deutschen Nationalbibliografie; detaillierte bibliografische Daten sind im Internet über http://dnb.d-nb.de abrufbar.
Alle in diesem Buch genannten Marken und Produktnamen unterliegen warenzeichen-, marken- oder patentrechtlichem Schutz bzw. sind Warenzeichen oder eingetragene Warenzeichen der jeweiligen Inhaber. Die Wiedergabe von Marken, Produktnamen, Gebrauchsnamen, Handelsnamen, Warenbezeichnungen u.s.w. in diesem Werk berechtigt auch ohne besondere Kennzeichnung nicht zu der Annahme, dass solche Namen im Sinne der Warenzeichen- und Markenschutzgesetzgebung als frei zu betrachten wären und daher von jedermann benutzt werden dürften.

Coverbild: www.purestockx.com

Verlag: VDM Verlag Dr. Müller Aktiengesellschaft & Co. KG
Dudweiler Landstr. 125 a, 66123 Saarbrücken, Deutschland
Telefon +49 681 9100-698, Telefax +49 681 9100-988, Email: info@vdm-verlag.de

Herstellung in Deutschland:
Schaltungsdienst Lange o.H.G., Zehrensdorfer Str. 11, D-12277 Berlin
Books on Demand GmbH, Gutenbergring 53, D-22848 Norderstedt
Reha GmbH, Dudweiler Landstr. 99, D- 66123 Saarbrücken
ISBN: 978-3-639-02779-2

Imprint (only for USA, GB)
Bibliographic information published by the Deutsche Nationalbibliothek: The Deutsche Nationalbibliothek lists this publication in the Deutsche Nationalbibliografie; detailed bibliographic data are available in the Internet at http://dnb.d-nb.de.
Any brand names and product names mentioned in this book are subject to trademark, brand or patent protection and are trademarks or registered trademarks of their respective holders. The use of brand names, product names, common names, trade names, product descriptions etc. even without
a particular marking in this works is in no way to be construed to mean that such names may be regarded as unrestricted in respect of trademark and brand protection legislation and could thus be used by anyone.

Cover image: www.purestockx.com

Publisher:
VDM Verlag Dr. Müller Aktiengesellschaft & Co. KG
Dudweiler Landstr. 125 a, 66123 Saarbrücken, Germany
Phone +49 681 9100-698, Fax +49 681 9100-988, Email: info@vdm-verlag.de

Copyright © 2008 VDM Verlag Dr. Müller Aktiengesellschaft & Co. KG and licensors
All rights reserved. Saarbrücken 2008

Produced in USA and UK by:
Lightning Source Inc., 1246 Heil Quaker Blvd., La Vergne, TN 37086, USA
Lightning Source UK Ltd., Chapter House, Pitfield, Kiln Farm, Milton Keynes, MK11 3LW, GB
BookSurge, 7290 B. Investment Drive, North Charleston, SC 29418, USA
ISBN: 978-3-639-02779-2

ACKNOWLEDGEMENTS

The title of this book is, in part, a quotation of Chief Crowfoot's statement prior to signing Treaty 7. The full quotation is located in Chapter 5.

I would like to acknowledge the contributions and influence of numerous people to the completion of this work in no particular order: Dr. Frank Tough for teaching me academic rigour; Dr. Harold Cardinal who continues to be an inspiration although no longer in the physical realm; my hundreds of students who have challenged me; my mother and father Orville and Helen Beisel for their patience and for relieving me of my household duties so I could write; Deryn Lewis for her editorial comments; Dawn Maurice for her formatting assistance; Dr. Beth Bilson and Sakej Henderson for their patience, understanding, and direction; Dr. John Borrows for his thorough reading of my thesis and his kind and insightful comments; Drs. Cora Voyageur and Evelyn Field for their encouragement and support; Dr. Harvey Scott and the Keepers of the Water for making this task worthwhile; and most especially my four children for whom this book is written and who patiently waited for me to take a real holiday for 5 years.

DEDICATION

To Nipi-achahk, in gratitude, for blessing us all.

TABLE OF CONTENTS

CHAPTER ONE: INTRODUCTION 1

1. Importance of the Topic 1
2. Scope of Research 2
3. Chapter Outline 3

CHAPTER TWO: ALBERTA'S CONSULTATION POLICY 5

2. What is Adequate Consultation? 7
3. The Principles of Constitutionalism and the Rule of Law 7
   3.1 Who Owes the Duty to Consult? 9
      3.1.1 Third Party Consultation 10
   3.2 When Does the Duty to Consult Arise? 11
      3.2.1 Consultation as Managing the Treaty Relationship 13
   3.3 Characteristics of Consultation 14
   3.4 What is the Range of Consultation Required? 14
      3.4.1 Consultation at the Low End of the Spectrum 17
      3.4.2 Consultation at the High End of the Spectrum 18
   3.5 First Nations Obligations in the Consultation Process 19

4. Accommodation 19

5. Alberta's Consultation Guidelines 21
   5.1 Alberta Environment's First Nation Consultation Guidelines 22
   5.2 Process Under the Guidelines 23

6. Consultation Under the *Water Act* 26
   6.1 The Water for Life Strategy 26
      6.1.1 Alberta's Water Consultation Process 26
      6.1.2 Highlights of Alberta's Water Policy 28
   6.2 The South Saskatchewan River Basin Water Management Plan 32

7. Conclusion 33

CHAPTER THREE: RECONCILIATION AND CONSULTATION 34

1. Introduction 34

2. Reconciliation Evolving in Constitutional Law 35
   2.1 *Sparrow*: Federal Power to be Reconciled with Federal Duty 36
   2.2 *Van der Peet*: Reconciling Prior Occupation with Crown Sovereignty and Reconciling Aboriginal Legal Perspectives and British Legal Perspectives 36
   2.3 *Gladstone* and *Delgamu'ukw*: Reconciliation of Aboriginal Societies with the Broader Political Community 38
   2.4 Madame Justice Mclachlin's Alternative View of Reconciliation 39
   2.5 *Haida*: Reconciliation as Balance and Compromise 44

3.	Checks and Balances on Consultation and Reconciliation	44
4.	*Mikisew*: Reconciliation as "Managing" the Treaty Relationship	46
5.	Does Reconciliation Require Limitations on Aboriginal Rights?	47
6.	How has Reconciliation Occurred to Date?	49
	6.1 The Peigan Water Use Agreement	49
	6.2 Alberta's *Water Act* and Water for Life Strategy	51
7.	Conclusion	54

CHAPTER FOUR: ABORIGINAL RIGHTS AND TITLE TO WATER — 57

1.	Introduction	57
2.	The Test for Identifying Aboriginal Rights protected by Section 35(1)	57
	2.1 Step One: Identify the Precise Nature of the Claim	58
	2.2 Step two: Central significance of Practices, Customs, and Traditions	60
	2.2.1 Continuity of the Claimed Right with Pre-contact Practice	63
	2.2.2 Site-specific Rights	64
3.	The Test for Establishing Aboriginal Title to the Waterbeds in Southern Alberta	65
	3.1 Occupation at the Time of Assertion of Sovereignty	66
	3.1.1 Occupation…	67
	3.1.2 …at the date of sovereignty	69
	3.2 Continuity of Occupation	70
	3.2.1 Internal Limits	71
	3.3 Exclusive Occupation at the Time of Sovereignty	71
4.	Conclusion	73

CHAPTER FIVE: THE EFFECT OF TREATY 7 ON WATER RIGHTS — 75

1.	Introduction	75
2.	What is the Meaning of Treaty 7?	77
	2.1 The Principles of Treaty Interpretation	77
	2.2 Historical Context of Treaty 7	78
	2.2.1 Treaty 7 First Nations Understanding	83
	2.2.2 The Federal Crown's perspective on the purpose of Treaty 7	84
	2.3 Application of the Principles of Treaty Interpretation to Treaty 7	87
3.	Did Treaty 7 Extinguish Aboriginal Rights and Title to Water?	88
	3.1 Extinguishment of Aboriginal Title	88
	3.1.1 Test for Extinguishment of Aboriginal Title	89
	3.1.2 Did the Cession of Land Include Title to the Riverbeds?	91
	3.1.3 Title to Water, Waterbeds and Watercourses Runs Separately from the land	91
	3.2 Extinguishment of Aboriginal Rights	95
4.	Rights to Water Under Treaty 7	96
	4.1 The Treaty Right to a Livelihood	97
	4.1.1 The Treaty Right to a Traditional Livelihood	97
	4.1.2 The Treaty Right to a Modern Livelihood	98

	4.2	The Treaty Right to a Reserve	100
	4.2.1	The Treaty Right to Water Appurtenant to a Reserve	100
	4.2.2	The Crown's Assumption of Title to Navigable Streams	105
5.	Conclusion		107

CHAPTER SIX: EXTINGUISHMENT OF ABORIGINAL AND TREATY RIGHTS BY FEDERAL LEGISLATION, CROWN ACTION, OR CROWN POLICY   109

1.	Introduction		109
	1.1	Extinguishment by Crown Action, Crown Policy, or Legislation	109
	1.1.1	Extinguishment by Crown Policy and Crown Action	110
	1.1.2	Extinguishment by Legislation	110
2.	Did the *North-West Irrigation Act* Extinguish Aboriginal and Treaty Rights to Water?		112
	2.1	Early Treatment of Treaty 7 First Nations Title to Water	114
3.	Did the *NRTA* Extinguish Aboriginal and Treaty Rights to Water?		116
	3.1	Principles for Interpreting the *NRTA*	117
	3.1.1	The Purpose of *NRTA* s.12	118
	3.1.2	The Effect of the *NRTA* on Treaty 7 First Nations' Water Rights	121
4.	Were Aboriginal and treaty rights extinguished by the *Water Resources Act* or the *Water Act*?		129
5.	Conclusion		130

CHAPTER SEVEN: CONCLUSION   132

1. Questions for Further Research   135

ADDENDUM: RECENT DEVELOPMENTS IN THE LAW IN ALBERTA   138

BIBLIOGRAPHY   144

Statutes   144

Treaties and Agreements   144

Case Law   144

Secondary Sources   148

LIST OF FIGURES

Figure 2-1. Groundwater Allocations in Alberta by Specific Use 6

Figure 2-2. The South Saskatchewan River Basin 28

Figure 4-1. The body of Napi 67

CHAPTER ONE: INTRODUCTION

The waters of the South Saskatchewan River Basin have been fully allocated under Alberta's water licencing regime, with less than .1% having been allocated to First Nations. This book strives to answer the question: What is the legal basis for the duty to consult with Treaty 7 First Nations on issues relating to water resources? Because the depth of consultation depends on the strength of the legal obligation to consult, each chapter focuses on one form of s.35 Aboriginal right. The legal basis for consultation with Treaty 7 First Nations on water issues, include reconciliation, unextinguished title, unextinguished aboriginal rights, Treaty rights, and rights under the NRTA. Each chapter applies the analysis of the existence of the legal basis for the duty to consult in the context of Treaty 7, describes the scope of the duty to consult based on the application of the law to the facts, and analyses whether the duty to consult has been met by the present provincial legal regime. In the final chapter, I will attempt to describe what constitutes adequate consultation.

1. Importance of the Topic

In Alberta's overheated economy, consultation with First Nations is one of the hottest topics in policy-making regarding natural resources generally and water resources in particular. To date there is no national standard for consultation with Aboriginal people. In an effort to meet the Supreme Court's requirements for Crown consultation, the Alberta government has devised a framework and guidelines for consultation which places the onus on proponents such as industry developers and municipal governments to consult. First Nations resist attending meetings with representatives of industry or municipalities for fear that it might be construed as consultation. It's a Mexican stand-off over water with all parties acknowledging that something must be done to address the province's dwindling freshwater resources and no-one daring to move forward.

Running parallel to Alberta's consultation process is the management of watersheds through watershed policy and advisory councils (WPACs). Under Alberta's Water for Life Policy implemented pursuant to the *Water Act*, WPACs are formed for each watershed area. Membership on WPACs is made up of "stakeholders" who attend meetings voluntarily. In theory, WPACs create and analyze policies that directly affect stakeholders and interests groups living within the watershed. Water management plans created by WPACs, such as the South

Saskatchewan River Basin Water Management Plan, will ideally be approved by the province after review. There is no obligation for WPACs to consider Aboriginal and Treaty rights and participation by First Nations in decision-making by WPACs is not mandatory. The subject of shared governance of water resources is being hotly debated by members of the Alberta Water Council: Some say WPACs have failed and there needs to be another, more effective, means to govern water resources.

This book suggests that Alberta has devised a legal regime that circumvents the treaty relationship between the Crown and Treaty 7 First Nations. Section 52 of the Constitution and the principles of constitutionalism and the rule of law require that Crown legislation and action must be consistent with the Constitution. Because Aboriginal and treaty rights are protected under s.35(1) of the Constitution, Alberta's consultation guidelines must address the protection of existing Aboriginal and treaty rights. This thesis examines whether the treaty or any subsequent Crown legislation or Crown action has extinguished the Aboriginal and treaty rights of Treaty 7 First Nations and draws the conclusion that the Aboriginal rights of Treaty 7 First Nations not only continue to exist, but are afforded additional protection by Treaty 7 and the *Natural Resources Transfer Agreement*. This leads to the conclusion that Alberta's consultation policy, failing to recognize and affirm Aboriginal and treaty rights in their entirety as they currently exist, is inconsistent with s.35(1) and are null and void.

2. Scope of Research

I limited my research to examining existing case law and secondary sources. Ideally, I would have liked to interview individuals involved in negotiations regarding water resources, but I when I approached members of Treaty 7 First Nations Councils for an interview, I was denied by their counsel. Clearly, these issues are sensitive, so out of respect, I have limited my research almost entirely to published materials. I have relied on my own experience as a member of the Bow River Basin Council Legislation and Policy Committee for information about the workings of Watershed Policy and Advisory Councils. I have no doubt that my conclusions would have been influenced by the views Treaty 7 First Nation members had I been able to interview them.

I am conscious that individuals involved in the area of watershed management are at least aware of Aboriginal and Treaty rights to water. Many of the people I have met know that there is a duty to consult, but do not know the degree of consultation that is required or how to meet this obligation. There is a fair amount of resentment among stakeholders that the province has devolved the obligation to consult to ordinary Albertans. The people that I have met appear to be trying to do their best without any guidance from Alberta Environment. Even individuals working within Alberta Environment are aware of the problems surrounding consultation with First Nations, but feel powerless to do anything without direction from the Minister. When I have referred to the Alberta Environment's failures to consult, I am referring to the Minister of Environment. It is my hope that some of my findings may shed some light on how WPACs might more effectively engage Treaty 7 First Nations in watershed governance.

3. **Chapter Outline**

Chapter Two summarizes the law of consultation and applies the standard set by leading case law to Alberta's current consultation policy. This chapter considers which parties owe a duty to consult, when the duty to consult arises, how consultation is part of the process of managing the Treaty relationship, the range of consultation required, and First Nations' obligations in the consultation process. Alberta's consultation guidelines developed for industry and Alberta Environment (AENV) use are analyzed as well as Alberta's Water for Life Policy which mandates the formation of WPACs for watershed management.

Chapter Three considers the duty to consult arising from the goal of reconciliation which is the over-arching purpose of s.35 of the Constitution Act, 1985. The definition of reconciliation has evolved over time from it initial inception in *Sparrow* which defined it as reconciliation of federal power with federal duty. *Van der Peet* expanded the definition of reconciliation to include reconciling prior occupation by Aboriginal peoples with Crown sovereignty and reconciling Aboriginal legal perspectives with British legal perspectives. The concept of reconciliation was broadened further in *Gladstone* and *Delgamu'ukw* to include reconciliation of Aboriginal societies with the broader political community. The Supreme Court in Haida described reconciliation as balance and compromise. Most importantly, for Treaty First Nations, *Mikisew* introduced the idea of reconciliation as an on-going process of managing the Treaty relationship. Chapter one critiques the characterization of reconciliation and suggests that the majority view in the leading cases leads to the erosion of Treaty rights by applying a balancing of interests analysis. The legal principles arising from the leading Supreme Court cases are applied to the Peigan Irrigation Agreement and the Water for Life Strategy as examples of the process of reconciliation.

Chapter Four indentifies the Blackfoot Confederacy's Aboriginal rights and title existing at the time of Treaty 7. The tests for indentifying Aboriginal rights and title protected by s.35(1) of the Constitution are applied.

Chapter Five consider the effect of Treaty 7 on the Aboriginal rights and title possessed by the Blackfoot Confederacy at the time of treaty signing. Applying the principles of Treaty interpretation, Treaty 7 and the historical context of the terms of Treaty 7 are briefly analyzed. The chapter considers whether Aboriginal water rights and title to water and waterbeds were extinguished or altered by Treaty 7.

Chapter Six assesses whether the Aboriginal and treaty rights of Treaty 7 First Nations were extinguished by legislation, Crown policy, or Crown action. Applying the principles for interpreting constitutional documents, the purpose and effect of the *NRTA* is examined, including the creation of trust obligations, the geographical expansion of livelihood rights, incidental rights, and lands to which Indians have a right of access

Finally, Chapter Seven draws the conclusion that Treaty 7 First Nations remain in possession of their original Aboriginal rights and title which have been afforded additional protection by Treaty 7 and the NRTA, thus Alberta's consultation policy must recognize and affirm them in their full vigour in order to be consistent with s.35(1) of the Constitution. This chapter also suggests areas of future study.

CHAPTER TWO: ALBERTA'S CONSULTATION POLICY

1. INTRODUCTION

Section 35 of the *Constitution Act, 1982*[1] protects existing and "potential" Aboriginal rights, obligating the Crown, by its honour, to determine, recognize and respect those rights, and participate in processes of negotiation. "While this process continues, the honour of the Crown may require it to consult and, where indicated, accommodate Aboriginal interests."[2] While consultation is the Crown's responsibility, third-party stakeholders such as the oil and gas industry, agricultural operations, and urban municipalities may be required to consult directly with Treaty 7 First Nations on use of water for economic purposes. The ultimate responsibility for ensuring that meaningful and substantial consultation takes place rests with the Crown.

While it is arguable that First Nations have Aboriginal and treaty rights to water, First Nations have few if any water licences:[3] When the *North-west Irrigation Act*[4] was passed, the Department of Indian Affairs did not see the utility in maintaining their water licences and allowed them to lapse. There are now no "new" allocations of water resources in the South Saskatchewan River Basin.

In the province of Alberta, the oil and gas industry has been allocated more than one quarter of all the fresh groundwater allocated in the province.[5] Most of the water used for oilfield injection turns saline and does not re-enter the hydrologic cycle. This practice may have an impact on water quantity and ultimately affect fish and wildlife ecosystems that will, in turn, diminish the supply of fish and game that make possible the exercise of Aboriginal and treaty rights.

---

[1] *Constitution Act, 1982*, being Schedule B to the *Canada Act 1982* (U.K.), 1982, c. 11 [hereinafter *Constitution Act, 1982*].

[2] *Haida Nation* v. *British Columbia (Minister of Forests)*, [2004] 3 S.C.R. 511; [2004] S.C.J. No. 70 (Q.L.); 2004 SCC 73 at para. 25 [hereinafter *Haida*].

[3] Jim Big Plume, Land Department, Tsuu T'ina Nation, informed me that the Tsuu T'ina Nation has a licence to extract .075% of the water from the Bow River. I was not able to verify this fact.

[4] *North-West Territories Act*, R.S.C. 1886, c. 50.

[5] Mary Griffiths and Dan Woynillowicz, *Oil and Troubled Waters: Reducing the impact of the oil and gas industry on Alberta's water resources*. (Pembina Institute).

In southern Alberta, the other major use of surface and groundwater is for irrigation agriculture. Irrigation Districts have ownership of a large proportion of the available water licences and are currently transferring some of those licences to municipalities whose development depends on the long-term availability of fresh water.[6]

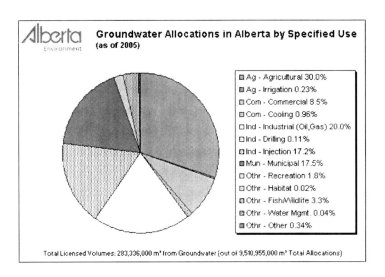

Figure 2-1. Groundwater Allocations in Alberta by Specific Use

The current allocation scheme and consequent environmental degradation presents a problem for the Crown: The water policy of the provincial Crown is inconsistent with the Crown's vested duty to conserve game under Treaty 7 and to conserve fish and game under the terms of the Natural Resources Transfer Agreements[7] that protect Indian livelihood.

Treaty 7 First Nations have only had minimal involvement in the drafting of Alberta's Consultation Guidelines and Water for Life Strategy, and no participation in drafting the South Saskatchewan River Basin Water Management Plan, the purpose of which is to strike a balance

---

[6] See Figure 2-1 (above) and Figure2-2 on page 38.
http://www3.gov.ab.ca/env/water/GWSW/quantity/waterinalberta/allocation/AL3_purpose.html, access on-line August 11, 2007.

[7] *Natural Resources Transfer Agreements*, being Schedules to the *Constitution Act, 1930* (U.K.), 20-21 George V, c.26 [*NRTA*].

between environmental protection and water allocation and use. These approved policies comprise the regime for water use, allocation, and consultation for regulatory approvals. It is the writer's opinion that while these policies may meet the province's conception of the legal requirements for consultation and accommodation, Alberta's water policies fall far short of the constitutional requirements for meaningful and substantial consultation. This chapter summarizes the constitutional requirements for consultation and applies these standards to Alberta's Consultation Guidelines and Water for Life strategy to determine how consultation processes in Alberta measure up to the Supreme Court's standards.

2. What is Adequate Consultation?

Subsequent chapters will examined in detail whether Aboriginal rights to water, which existed prior to contact and at various stages of colonization, survived the assertion of Crown sovereignty to be classified as what we now recognize as Aboriginal rights, Aboriginal title, Treaty rights, and livelihood rights as protected by the *NRTA*. I have concluded in the chapters following that no imperial acts to date have effectively extinguished the entire bundle of Treaty 7 First Nations' water rights. Given that even the potential existence of some form of Aboriginal right to water triggers the duty to consult, the Crown clearly has a duty to consult with Treaty 7 First Nations regarding the use of the waters within Treaty 7 territories. Below is a brief summary of the consultation requirements.[8]

3. The Principles of Constitutionalism and the Rule of Law

The standard used to determine the adequacy of consultation is whether consultation has been "consistent with the honour of the Crown."[9] This test has developed as it has largely because it is retrospective, assessing past conduct at the justificatory stage of the *Sparrow* analysis. The Court has perhaps not had the opportunity to consider the larger question of whether recently developed provincial or federal regulations governing the constitutional process are consistent with the Constitution.

---

[8] An analysis of what constitutes meaningful and substantial consultation is worthy of a thesis in and of itself. The purpose of this section is merely to summarize the main requirements set out by the Supreme Court.

[9] *Mikisew Cree First Nation* v. *Canada (Minister of Canadian Heritage)*, [2005] S.C.J. No. 71 (QL); 2005 SCC 69 at para. 67 [hereinafter *Mikisew*], *Haida*, *supra* note 2 at para. 38.

Section 52 of the Canadian Constitution[10] reads:

> (1) The Constitution of Canada is the supreme law of Canada, and any law that is inconsistent with the provisions of the Constitution is, to the extent of the inconsistency, of no force or effect.

In the Quebec Secession Reference, the Supreme Court explained that

> The essence of constitutionalism in Canada is embodied in s. 52(1) of the Constitution Act, 1982, which provides that "[t]he Constitution of Canada is the supreme law of Canada, and any law that is inconsistent with the provisions of the Constitution is, to the extent of the inconsistency, of no force or effect."[11]

It has been argued that the Treaties form part of the law of Canada and, indeed, are constitutional documents.[12] If that is the case, then any government consultation must also be consistent with the treaties.

Like the constitutionalism principle, "[t]he rule of law principle requires that all government action must comply with the law, including the Constitution."[13]

Having transformed the Canadian system of government

> from a system of Parliamentary supremacy to one of constitutional supremacy. The Constitution binds all governments, both federal and provincial, including the executive branch (reference omitted). They may not transgress its provisions: indeed, <u>their sole claim to exercise lawful authority rests in the powers allocated to them under the Constitution, and can come from no other source</u> (emphasis mine).[14]

The only lawful authority for the provincial government to regulate resource use is the Constitution and its package of constitutional documents including the Treaties and the *NRTA*. Thus, the process of consultation, negotiation, and reconciliation must consider what lawful authority is vested in the provincial Crown as well as what residual Aboriginal and Treaty rights exist in the context of the various constitutional documents. If all government action must comply with the Constitution, then provincial consultation policies must be consistent not only with the s.35(1) protection of Aboriginal rights, but also with the treaties.

---

[10] *Constitution Act 1982, supra* note 1.

[11] *Reference re Secession of Quebec*, [1998] S.C.J. No. 61 (QL); [1998] 2 S.C.R. 217 at para. 72 [hereinafter *Quebec Reference*].

[12] James [Sákéj] Youngblood Henderson, "Empowering Treaty Federalism" (1994) Saskatchewan Law Review 158.

[13] Ibid.

[14] *Quebec Reference, supra* note 11, quoting *Operation Dismantle Inc.* v. *The Queen*, [1985] 1 S.C.R. 441, at p. 455.

Indeed, if the province refuses to negotiate "in a manner consistent with constitutional principles and values" the province puts at risk the legitimacy of claim to jurisdiction over water resources "and perhaps the negotiation process as a whole."[15] The constitutionalism principle implies that the province must be consistent with the mandated protection of existing Aboriginal and treaty rights and the Crown's obligations under Treaty 7 and the *NRTA*: The legitimacy of Crown jurisdiction would be called into question if it merely assumed that all Aboriginal and treaty rights have been extinguished by treaty or statute, giving the provincial Crown unfettered jurisdiction over water resources.

The province of Alberta has done exactly what it cannot legitimately do under the constitutionalism principle. The province assumed that all Aboriginal rights and title to water have been extinguished leaving no residual water rights to Treaty 7 First Nations. The provincial Crown then passed the *Water Act,* enacted a regulatory regime governing water resource planning and allocation, and created consultation guidelines that devolve responsibility for consultation to third party industries, all without seriously contemplating the Treaty relationship and the obligations and jurisdictions arising therefrom.

3.1   Who Owes the Duty to Consult?

The Crown, not industry, is charged with the duty to consult with First Nations on proposed developments. In *Haida*, the terms of the tree harvesting licence approved for Weyerhaeuser mandated the company to specify what measures that it would take to identify and consult with aboriginal people claiming an aboriginal interest in or to the area. The Court recognized that, while the Crown is ultimately responsible for consultation, the procedural details of consultation may be delegated to industry. Given that "the duty to consult and accommodate...flows from the Crown's assumption of sovereignty over lands and resources formerly held by the Aboriginal group" the Crown is solely responsible for consultation and accommodation. The Crown is also legally responsible for "the consequences of its actions and interactions with third parties that affect Aboriginal interests." However, "[t]he Crown may delegate procedural aspects of consultation to industry proponents seeking a particular development; this is not infrequently done in environmental assessments."[16]

---

[15]   *Ibid.* at para. 95.

[16]   *Haida, supra* note 2 at para. 53.

Even though there is no requirement that third parties consult with or accommodate First Nations, it does not mean that "they can never be liable to Aboriginal peoples. If they act negligently in circumstances where they owe Aboriginal peoples a duty of care, or if they breach contracts with Aboriginal peoples or deal with them dishonestly, they may be held legally liable. But they cannot be held liable for failing to discharge the Crown's duty to consult and accommodate."[17] The Court very clearly stated that, although third parties may be involved in consultation with First Nations, "the ultimate legal responsibility for consultation and accommodation rests with the Crown. The honour of the Crown cannot be delegated" (emphasis mine).[18] Industry does not "owe any independent duty to consult with or accommodate" First Nations concerns, "although the possibility remains that it could become liable for assumed obligations."[19]

If responsibility for consultation cannot be delegated, the determination of what constitutes adequate or appropriate consultation cannot be left to the discretion of third parties. The Crown is ultimately responsible for determining the procedural requirements of consultation and for monitoring the quality of consultation, even if the actual consultation is carried out by third parties. Anything less would be an abdication of the Crown's duty. Alberta has, by establishing Consultation Guidelines, attempted to discharge the Crown's duty to consult and devolve responsibility for developing consultation plans to third party industries such as forestry, mining, and oil extraction and processing.

3.1.1 Third Party Consultation

Although it was determined in Haida that "[t]he duty to consult and, if appropriate, accommodate cannot be discharged by delegation"[20] to third parties, it is Alberta's official policy for all resource industries to consult with First Nations, particularly in the oil industry, as there may be live issues with regard to 'rights and traditional uses' of land within the territories being exploited for oil resources. This policy would constitute a prohibited delegation of the Crown's obligation, particularly in the treaty context in which there is a clear relationship between the

---

[17]   *Ibid.* at para. 56.
[18]   *Ibid.* at para. 53.
[19]   *Ibid.* at para. 10.
[20]   *Ibid.*

Crown and Treaty 7 First Nations. Nonetheless, Alberta takes the position that it has discharged its duty to consult by setting consultation policy. It is unclear what constitutes adequate consultation by industry with First Nations as there are few decisions on point.

Some communities have consultation agreements guiding their communications with industry, while others do not. For example, the Wood Buffalo First Nation opposed a Steam-Assisted Gravity Drainage (SAGD) Project operation stating that insufficient information was available to assess underground water systems and potential contamination of the MacKay River and natural springs. They were not opposed to the project *per se*, providing there was sufficient environmental testing and mitigation. Wood Buffalo requested a consultation agreement with Petro-Canada to address the concerns of its members because the MacKay River project would be on its traditional lands, and to facilitate meaningful consultation so that the First Nation could give its full support to the project. The Alberta Energy and Utilities Board determined that Petro-Canada's consultation program led to effective and meaningful communication between the parties.[21] The "progressive approach" employed by Petro-Canada "established relationships that should continue to produce positive results by promoting a shared understanding of both technical and social issues that are important to [First Nations] stakeholders."[22]

It is clear from the discussion below that Alberta's consultation guidelines that Crown Alberta has taken control over establishing standards for consultation while devolving responsibility for consultation to industry proponents.

3.2   When Does the Duty to Consult Arise?

In the context of a proposed development, there is potential for conflict over the determination of when consultation must take place. Generally, the duty to consult arises from the Crown's honour and the goal of reconciliation. Consultation must take place "when the Crown has knowledge, real or constructive, of the potential existence of the Aboriginal right or

---

[21]   The AEUB's ability to consider constitutional questions may be a double-edged sword: One side, it allows First Nations to submit Statements of Concern to the AEUB based on failure to engage in meaningful and substantial consultation, thus preserving their rights to future appeals on other than purely scientific grounds, but on the other side, it allows the AEUB, a creature of provincial statute, to determine constitutional rights which may render First Nations vulnerable to the erosion of their rights through bad precedent.

[22]   Petro-Canada Oil and Gas Steam-Assisted Gravity Drainage Project Mackay River Project Athabasca Oil Sands Area, Decision 2000-50, Application No. 1032550.

title and contemplates conduct that might adversely affect it."[23] There is a legal duty to consult "prior to proof of claims" and "<u>before</u> determination of the right."[24] Proof of the right is not the trigger for a legal duty to consult and accommodate "even in the context of justification."[25]

The court suggests that any knowledge "of a credible but unproven claim" is sufficient to trigger a duty to consult and accommodate, however, the scope of the duty will vary with the situation: If a claim is "dubious," "peripheral," or "tenuous" a "mere duty of notice" may suffice. The parties themselves should "assess these matters, and if they cannot agree, tribunals and courts can assist. Difficulties associated with the absence of proof and definition of claims are addressed by assigning appropriate content to the duty, not by denying the existence of a duty."[26]

Clearly, the duty to consult arises when Aboriginal "interests are being seriously pursued in the process of treaty negotiation and proof."[27] The *Haida* situation arose in the context of unresolved land claims. There it was determined that in such a situation, although the Crown is not "rendered impotent" during the process of Treaty negotiations, the Crown, "acting honourably, cannot cavalierly run roughshod over Aboriginal interests":

> It may continue to manage the resource in question pending claims resolution. But, depending on the circumstances, discussed more fully below, the honour of the Crown may require it to consult with and reasonably accommodate Aboriginal interests pending resolution of the claim. To unilaterally exploit a claimed resource during the process of proving and resolving the Aboriginal claim to that resource, may be to deprive the Aboriginal claimants of some or all of the benefit of the resource. That is not honourable.[28]

The federal and provincial Crowns have an obligation to consult with Treaty 7 First Nations concerning the possible impacts of developments on their Treaty and Aboriginal rights upon the First Nation asserting a credible but unproven claim to the existence of such a right. The assertion of the claim will put the Crown on notice as to the possible existence of the right, and will trigger a duty on the part of the Crown to make further reasonable inquiry. While the

---

[23] *Haida, supra* note 2 at para. 35, see *Halfway River First Nation v. British Columbia (Ministry of Forests)*, [1997] 4 C.N.L.R. 45 (B.C.S.C.), at para. 71, *per* Dorgan J.

[24] *Haida, ibid.*

[25] *Ibid.* at para. 34, *R. v. Sparrow*, [1990] 1 S.C.R. 1075; [1990] S.C.J. No. 49, *R. v. Nikal*, [1996] 1 S.C.R. 1013; [1996] S.C.J. No. 47 (QL) [hereinafter *Sparrow*], and *R. v. Gladstone*, [1996] 2 S.C.R. 723; [1996] S.C.J. No. 79 (QL) [hereinafter *Gladstone*].

[26] *Haida, ibid.* at para. 37.

[27] *Ibid.* at para. 27.

[28] *Ibid.*

government is not required to consult regarding every development "no matter how remote or unsubstantial the impact,"[29]

In the treaty context, where First Nations clearly have a right to engage in traditional livelihood pursuits throughout a defined treaty territory, the Crown must "consult and, if appropriate, accommodate First Nations' interests before reducing the area over which their members may continue to pursue their hunting, trapping and fishing rights."[30] The court has made no determination regarding Treaty First Nations' proprietary rights to lands within the "ceded territory" in the context of a treaty. As we will see in Chapter Five, Treaty 7 First Nations may not have ceded their proprietary rights or jurisdiction over water. It is unclear what the scope of the duty to consult would be in such a situation.

3.2.1 Consultation as Managing the Treaty Relationship

Where there is a treaty relationship, it could be argued that the Crown has real or constructive knowledge that any development may adversely affect the Treaty rights of First Nation and impact the treaty relationship. In *Mikisew*, the Supreme Court held that consultation has an added element of "managing change" and "managing" the relationship between the Crown and First Nation.

The Supreme Court acknowledged that "[t]he Crown has a treaty right to "take up" surrendered lands." Where "the impacts [are] clear, established and demonstrably adverse to the continued exercise of the [First Nation] hunting and trapping rights over the lands in question, the Crown is "under an obligation to inform itself of the impact its project will have on the exercise" of those rights and to communicate its findings to the First Nation affected.[31] The Crown is obligated to deal with Treaty First Nations "in good faith, and with the intention of substantially addressing"[32] In Badger, which did not consider consultation directly, the Supreme Court held that in the context of infringement of Aboriginal rights under the *NRTA*, the special trust relationship and the responsibility of the government vis-à-vis the aboriginal people must be

---

[29] *Mikisew, supra* note 9 at para. 55.

[30] *Ibid.* at para. 56.

[31] *Ibid.* at para. 55.

[32] *Delgamu'ukw* v. *British Columbia*, [1997] S.C.J. No. 108 (QL); [1997] 3 S.C.R. 1010 at para. 168 [hereinafter *Delgamuukw*].

taken into consideration when deciding whether the aboriginal group was adequately consulted with respect to the conservation measures.[33]

3.3 Characteristics of Consultation

The characteristics of what would constitute adequate consultation are contextual and relative. The Supreme Court has set a basic standard by which to assess the adequacy of consultation, but have left the determination of the process to the parties themselves. The reason given is that reconciliation, of which consultation and accommodation are a part, is a political process in which the Courts do not have role other than to set basic standard for review if necessary.[34] The few decisions that exist have established that, while "consultation must be meaningful"[35] and substantive, "there is no duty to reach agreement,"[36] which appears to be contrary to the overarching purpose of s.35 to reconcile First Nations with the assertion of sovereignty. Consultation and accommodation "entails [the] balancing of Aboriginal and other interests."[37] The content of the duty varies with the circumstances: from a minimum "duty to discuss important decisions" where the "breach is less serious or relatively minor"; through to "significantly deeper than mere consultation" that is required in "most cases"; to "full consent of [the] aboriginal nation" on very serious issues."[38]

3.4 What is the Range of Consultation Required?

Generally, "the scope of the duty is proportionate to a preliminary assessment of the strength of the case supporting the existence of the right or title, and to the seriousness of the potentially adverse effect upon the right or title claimed."[39] The Court would prefer that the parties be able to assess the strength of the case or seriousness of the potential impact, but all too often, that is the fundamental point on which the parties have very divergent views. If it cannot

---

[33] *R. v. Badger*, [1996] 1 S.C.R. 771; [1996] S.C.J. No. 39 (QL) [hereinafter *Badger*] at para. 97, quoting *Sparrow, supra* note 25 at para.1114.

[34] This subject is more fully dealt with in chapter three.

[35] *Haida, supra* note 2 at para. 10.

[36] *Ibid.*

[37] *Ibid.* at para. 14.

[38] *Ibid.* at para. 24.

[39] *Ibid.* at para. 39.

be resolved consensually, the only recourse is to take the question to Co⎯ consultation guidelines reflect the province's view that treaty First Nations posses⎯ ⎯⎯⎯ ⎯⎯ engage in traditional activities, not land or water rights. First Nations maintain that they have residual title to their lands and waters within their traditional territories.

Clearly, the scope and content of the duty to consult is dependent on context. What is required of the government may vary with the strength of the claim and the circumstances.[40] The duty to consult is triggered at a low threshold, but "adverse impact is a matter of degree, as is the extent of the Crown's duty."[41] The more serious the impact the more important will be the role of consultation.[42] Thus the provincial government and industry must be diligent in consulting with First Nations on the strength of their claims as well as the seriousness of the adverse impact of all proposed projects. If the province or developers fail in their assessment, this would be grounds for administrative review by the Alberta Energy and Utilities Board (AEUB)[43] or by the judiciary.

The history of the relationship between the Crown and the First Nation may also be a significant factor in determining the level of consultation required.[44] The Supreme Court stated in *Mikisew*, that where specific Treaty promises have been made, "the role of consultation may be quite limited."[45] This dicta seems to contradict the Supreme Court's decision in *Delagmu'ukw* where it was determined the full consent of First Nations may be required, particularly when hunting and fishing may be adversely affected.[46]

While all parties would have liked the Supreme Court to have set specific guidelines, the Court felt it is "not useful to classify situations into watertight compartments," as different situations require different responses. "In all cases, the honour of the Crown requires that the

---

[40] *Ibid.* at para. 38.

[41] *Mikisew, supra* note 9 at para 55.

[42] *Ibid.* at para. 63.

[43] The AEUB has been divided into the Alberta Utilities Commission and Alberta Energy Board. The AEUB has been conferred the power to consider constitutional matters provided they were referenced in a Statement of Concern. The Environmental Appeals Board, the board responsible for most *Water Act* approvals, does not have such power.

[44] *Mikisew, supra* note 9 at para. 63.

[45] *Ibid.*

[46] *Delgamuukw, supra* note 32 at para. 168.

Crown act with good faith to provide meaningful consultation appropriate to the circumstances"[47] with a view to substantially addressing First Nations' concerns as they are raised through a meaningful process of consultation.[48]

The fact that consultation may be inconvenient or cause delay does not weaken the Crown's obligation. In *R. v. Noel*,[49] the court held that the short time frame required for a decision to establish a hunting corridor did not entitle the Northwest Territories Government to overlook the rights of First Nations:

> Consultation must require the government to carry out <u>meaningful and reasonable discussions</u> with the representatives of Aboriginal people involved. <u>The fact that the time frame for action was short does not justify the government to push forward with their proposed regulation without proper consultation.</u>[50]

The Court has stated that

> Every case must be approached individually... flexibly, since the level of consultation required may change as the process goes on and new information comes to light. The controlling question in all situations is what is required to maintain the honour of the Crown and to effect reconciliation between the Crown and the Aboriginal peoples with respect to the interests at stake. Pending settlement, the Crown is bound by its honour to balance societal and Aboriginal interests in making decisions that may affect Aboriginal claims. The Crown may be required to make decisions in the face of disagreement as to the adequacy of its response to Aboriginal concerns. Balance and compromise will then be necessary.[51]

The parties must be committed to a meaningful process of consultation[52] that may not lead ultimately to agreement.[53] In the consultation process, sharp dealing is not permitted[54] but hard bargaining does not breach a First Nation's right to be consulted.[55] This is where the protection of Aboriginal rights under s.35 breaks down: Reconciliation may require consultation,

---

[47] *Haida, supra* note 2 at para. 41.

[48] *Delgamuukw, supra* note 32 at para. 168; *Haida, ibid.* at para. 42.

[49] *R. v. Noel*, [1995] 4 C.N.L.R. 78.

[50] *Ibid.*

[51] *Haida, supra* note 2 at para. 45.

[52] *Ibid.* at para. 42.

[53] *Ibid., Mikisew, supra* note 9 at para. 66.

[54] *Haida, supra* note 2 at para. 42.

[55] *Ibid.*

negotiation and bargaining, but if Aboriginal rights are capable of bargained into extinguishment without the consent of First Nations, the supremacy of the constitution is undermined.

The range of the Crown's duty to consult was considered in *Delgamu'ukw*. The Crown's duty ranges from "no more than a duty to discuss important decisions," to the obligation to "give notice, disclose information, and discuss any issues raised in response to the notice,"[56] to good faith consultation, and to obtain the full consent of the First Nation.[57]

In situations where a First Nation has a strong *prima facie* case, "the right and potential infringement is of high significance to the Aboriginal peoples, and the risk of non-compensable damage is high…deep consultation, aimed at finding a satisfactory interim solution, may be required."[58]

Haida and *Taku* discussed the indicia of adequate consultation and accommodation. In *Haida* the Court recognized that the potential adverse impacts were great and irreversible: The old growth forest was vital to the Haida economy and culture, and could never be replaced. Furthermore, the First Nation's claim of title to the Haida Gwaii was strong but would take many years to prove. In the mean time, if logging was not curtailed, "their heritage would be irretrievably despoiled."[59] In *Taku*, the same duty arose, but the Court found that the First Nation had been consulted and efforts had been made to accommodate their interests, thus the mining project could go forward despite the lack of agreement.

3.4.1 Consultation at the Low End of the Spectrum

At the low end of the spectrum, where the strength of the Aboriginal right claimed is relatively weak, the duty to consult may be confined to merely providing notice, information, and listening the First Nation's responses with a view to mitigating negative impacts on Aboriginal rights. Merely giving notice (such as posting an ad in the local newspaper) will not be sufficient. In *Mikisew*, the Supreme Court stated that the Crown must not only provide information about the project, but also address Aboriginal interests and potential adverse impact on those interests. This requires the Crown to keep itself well informed of the status of Aboriginal rights.

---

[56] *Ibid.* at para. 43.
[57] *Delgamuukw*, *supra* note 32 para. 168.
[58] *Haida*, *supra* note 2 at para. 44.
[59] *Ibid.* at para. 7.

Furthermore, the Crown is required to solicit and to listen carefully to the Aboriginal concerns, and to attempt to minimize adverse impacts on the First Nations' rights. The Crown must provide First Nations with "all necessary information in a timely way so that they have an opportunity to express their interests and concerns." Adequate notice is required "to ensure that their representations are seriously considered and, wherever possible, demonstrably integrated into the proposed plan of action."[60]

In *Mikisew*, the Supreme Court held that communications by the federal Minister of Environment in the form of "standard information about the proposed road in the same form and substance as the communications being distributed to the general public of interested stakeholders,"[61] along with open houses, was not adequate consultation.

3.4.2 Consultation at the High End of the Spectrum

In *Delgamu'ukw*, Chief Justice Lamer contemplated situations where First Nations consent may be required, particularly where the province's legislation may impact or infringe traditional hunting and fishing in an area where there was the existence of potential Aboriginal title. Qualifying the circumstances where veto power could be exercised, the Supreme Court in *Haida* denied that Aboriginal groups have a veto in [consultations] in situations where final proof of a claim to Aboriginal title is pending. Consent from Aboriginal groups in consultations is only required "in cases of established rights, and then by no means in every case.[62] Apparently contradicting that Court's earlier statement, the Supreme Court further stated, in *Mikisew*, that the duty to consult does not give veto power to First Nations.[63] This dicta appears to give an unfair veto power to the Crown in consultations in situations where agreement cannot be reached.

The Court clearly prefers a process of balancing interests approach to consultation: However, the balancing of interests risks the assimilation of Aboriginal peoples if the honour of the Crown and the process of reconciliation is not faithfully adhered to.

---

[60] *Halfway River*, supra note 23 at paras. 159-160; *Mikisew*, supra note 9 at para. 64.
[61] *Mikisew*, ibid. at paras. 9 and 20.
[62] *Haida*, supra note 2 at para. 48.
[63] *Mikisew*, supra note 9 at para. 66.

3.5 First Nations Obligations in the Consultation Process

The Crown needs to have "an idea of the asserted rights and of their strength trigger an obligation to consult and accommodate." To facilitate the Crown's knowledge, "claimants should outline their claims with clarity, focusing on the scope and nature of the Aboriginal rights they assert and on the alleged infringements."[64] If possible, the First Nation's assertion of right should be supported by evidence. This will not only serve to put the Crown on notice and trigger its duty to make further inquiries: It will also strengthen the scope of the consultation obligation owed by the Crown following assertion of the right. Aboriginal claimants must not frustrate the Crown's reasonable good faith attempts to consult with them.[65] First Nations should not take unreasonable positions to thwart the government from making decisions or acting in cases where, despite meaningful consultation, agreement is not reached.[66]

4. Accommodation

The Siamese twin of consultation is accommodation. The Supreme Court held in *Mikisew* that "[c]onsultation that excludes from the outset any form of accommodation would be meaningless." Consultation and accommodation is not simply a process "giving the Mikisew an opportunity to blow off steam before the Minister proceeds to do what she intended to do all along."[67] Rather, on-going consultation and accommodation is part of the "the long process of reconciliation" that began prior to Treaty-making. If the meaning of adequate and substantial consultation is unclear, the meaning of accommodation is doubly so. The concept of accommodation has been raised in cases such as *Sparrow, Sioui, Coté, Delgamu'ukw, Haida*, and *Mikisew* but the court has not fully developed the concept nor its requirements. Accommodation appears to require the balancing of competing societal interests with Aboriginal and Treaty rights[68] "in a manner which does not strain 'the Canadian legal and constitutional structure'"[69]

---

[64] *Haida, supra* note 2 at para. 36.

[65] *Ibid.* at para. 42.

[66] *Ibid.*; *Halfway River First Nation v. British Columbia (Ministry of Forests)*, [1999] 4 C.N.L.R. 1 (B.C.C.A.) at 44; *Heiltsuk Tribal Council v. British Columbia (Minister of Sustainable Resource Management)* (2003), 19 B.C.L.R. (4th) 107 (B.C.S.C.)

[67] *Mikisew, supra* note 1 at para. 54.

[68] *Sparrow, supra* note 25.

[69] *Delgamuukw, supra* note 32 at para. 82

Aboriginal societies are to be balanced with the broader political community by distributing resources fairly. Legitimate government objectives in enacting laws and setting policy regarding resource distribution includes "the pursuit of economic and regional fairness."[70] This balancing of interests approach seems to be inconsistent with the protection of Aboriginal peoples' s. 35 constitutional rights. Where the interests of the Crown and First nations appear to be at odds, the Crown bears the burden of proving that its occupancy of lands "cannot be accommodated to the reasonable exercise of [First Nations] rights."[71] Restrictions on Aboriginal rights may "be accommodated with the Crown's special fiduciary relationship with First Nations".[72] However, it appears that restrictions on constitutional rights contradict the constitutional fiduciary relationship of protection of rights with First Nation.

The Supreme Court appears to suggest that consultation be conducted in stages. The outcome of initial good faith consultation may be an obligation of the Crown to accommodate First Nations concerns.[73] Consultation may reveal that there is a strong *prima facie* case plus significant adverse effects, and thus accommodation is required to take "steps to avoid irreparable harm or to minimize the effects of infringement, pending final resolution of the underlying claim."[74] Clearly, consultation is not a linear process, as consultation that reveals the need for "... the process of accommodation of the treaty right [which] may best be resolved by consultation and negotiation."[75]

The Court grappled with the meaning of accommodation in *Haida*. With no cases in Canada regarding the nature and scope of accommodation, the Court looked to the Maori example.[76] Accommodation, the Court suggests entails gathering information to test policy proposals, putting forward proposals that are not yet finalized along with all relevant information upon which those proposals are based, seeking and listening to First Nations' opinions on those proposals, and being prepared to amend policy proposals in the light of information received, and

---

[70] *Ibid.* at para. 161.

[71] *R.* v. *Sioui*, [1990] 1 S.C.R. 1025 at para. 1072.

[72] *R.* v. *Coté*, [1996] S.C.J. No. 93; [1996] 3 S.C.R. 139; 138 D.L.R. (4th) 385; 202 N.R. 161; [1996] 4 C.N.L.R. 26 at para. 81.

[73] *Haida, supra* note 2 at para. 10.

[74] *Ibid.* at para. 47.

[75] *Ibid.*, citing *R.* v. *Marshall*, [1999] 3 S.C.R. 533, at para. 22.

[76] New Zealand Ministry of Justice's *Guide for Consultation with Maori* (1997) in *Haida, supra* note 2 at para 46 relied on by Alberta Department of Aboriginal Affairs in developing Alberta's Consultation Policy.

providing feedback."[77] The end result of meaningful consultation may be the conclusion that the Crown has obligation to accommodate First Nations by amending Crown policy.[78]

The Court defines accommodation as seeking to harmonize, balance, and reconcile conflicting interests. There is no duty to agree, but there is a requirement to make "good faith efforts to understand each other's concerns and move to address them."[79] The processes of reconciliation, consultation, negotiation, and ultimate accommodation, being essentially political, must nevertheless meet the standard of the principles of constitutionalism and the rule of law. That is, in so far a these political processes are government acts, they must be consistent with the s.35(1) protection of Aboriginal and treaty rights.

5. Alberta's Consultation Guidelines

It appears that Alberta has taken the Supreme Court's recommendation seriously and has fashioned its consultation policy as "deep consultation", setting out the process by which First Nations have "the opportunity to make submissions for consideration," "provision of written reasons to show that Aboriginal concerns were considered and to reveal the impact they had on the decision," complete with "dispute resolution procedures like mediation or administrative regimes with impartial decision-makers in complex or difficult cases."[80] Alberta's consultation policy does not include, however, "formal participation in the decision-making process" as recommended. However, as the Supreme Court cautioned, "[t]his list is neither exhaustive, nor mandatory for every case."[81]

The Supreme Court recommended in *Haida* that, to facilitate accommodation, provincial governments "set up regulatory schemes to address the procedural requirements appropriate to different problems at different stages."[82] By taking this pro-active approach it was hoped that the reconciliation process would be strengthened and there would be less recourse to the courts. Regulations could establish the consultation process, the minimum requirements in defined situations, and the roles and obligations of each party. Provincial governments "may not simply

---

[77] *Haida, ibid.*, quoting New Zealand Ministry of Justice's *Guide for Consultation with Maori* (1997).

[78] *Haida, ibid.*

[79] *Ibid.* at para. 49.

[80] *Ibid.* at para. 44.

[81] *Ibid.*

[82] *Ibid.* at para. 51.

adopt an unstructured discretionary administrative regime which risks infringing aboriginal rights in a substantial number of applications in the absence of some explicit guidance."[83]

British Columbia has had a Provincial Policy for Consultation with First Nations to direct the terms of provincial ministries' and agencies' operational guidelines. The Supreme Court noted that, although the policy fell short of a regulatory scheme, it provided a guide for decision-makers that prevented unstructured discretionary administrative decisions. Taking the recommendation of the Supreme Court to heart, Alberta Environment drafted its Consultation Policy and Guidelines, the final draft of which was publish in May, 2006. [84]

5.1 Alberta Environment's First Nation Consultation Guidelines

The government of Alberta's First Nations Consultation Policy on Land Management and Resource Development was approved May 16, 2005. This policy provided the basis upon which Alberta Environment developed its First Nation Consultation Guidelines[85] which was published for discussion purposes on May 18, 2006. The guiding principles for consultation excerpted from the policy include the following:

1. Consultation must be conducted in good faith.
2. Alberta is responsible for managing the consultation process.
3. Consultation will occur before decisions are made, where land management and resource development may infringe First Nations rights and traditional uses.
4. While each has very different roles, the consultation process requires the participation of First Nations, the project proponent and Alberta.
5. Alberta's consultation practices will be coordinated across departments.
6. Parties are expected to provide relevant information, allowing adequate time for the other parties to review it.

---

[83] *R.* v. *Adams*, [1996] 3 S.C.R. 101; 138 D.L.R. (4th) 657; 202 N.R. 89; 110 C.C.C. (3d) 97; [1996] 4 C.N.L.R. 1 at para. 54. Note that the infringement test is part of the reconciliation processes in *Sparrow*, but it is distinct process from consultation and accommodation as well as administrative decisions.

[84] Alberta Environment, "First Nation Consultation Guidelines (Regulatory Authorizations and Environmental Impact Assessments) Draft 1, May 18, 2006" accessed at http://www.aand.gov.ab.ca/AANDFlash/Files/AENV_FN_Guidelines_Draft_1_May_18_2006.pdf, on July 31, 2006, [hereinafter *Consultation Guidelines*]

[85] *Ibid.*

7. The nature of the consultation will depend on such factors potential infringement, the communities affected, and the nature involved.
8. Consultation should be conducted with the objective of avoiding infr...ent of First Nations rights and traditional uses. Where avoidance is not possible, consultation will be conducted with the goal of mitigating such infringement.
9. Consultation will occur within applicable legislative and regulatory timelines.

It is notable that Alberta's the Guidelines to not acknowledge the constitutional duty of consistency with aboriginal and treaty rights of Aboriginal peoples. All throughout Alberta's Consultation policies, the term "traditional uses" is used rather than "traditional land uses." It is not clear whether these "traditional uses" will be interpreted in their modern context or whether the provincial definition freezes them in time. By this term the policy framers mean to include uses of public lands such as burial grounds, gathering sites, and historic or ceremonial locations, and existing constitutionally protected Aboriginal, treaty, and *NRTA* rights to hunt, trap and fish and not proprietary interests in land, like aboriginal tenure or title. By focussing on "traditional uses," claims to unextinguished and unceded Aboriginal rights to water resources whether by virtue of title or of rights to water are side-stepped, which could be viewed as "sharp dealing" in a manner unbefitting of the Crown.

5.2 Process Under the Guidelines

Although third parties have no duty to consult with First Nations, the implementation of the Crown's duty to consult may be delegated to third parties. The ultimate legal responsibility for meeting the requirements of meaningful and substantial consultation rests with the Crown, as the honour of the Crown cannot be delegated. Alberta acknowledges that the province has a duty to consult and is accountable for consultations undertaken with First Nations where legislation, regulations or other actions have the potential to adversely impact Aboriginal and treaty rights, but it delegates some aspects of consultation to project proponents. This permanent delegation is neither valid nor legitimate, as project proponents have no treaty relationship with First Nations and owe no constitutional duties to Aboriginal peoples: The decision to delegate the responsibility for consultation is a matter of expediency. While the province accepts its role in managing consultation, it expects that project proponents will provide project-specific information to Alberta Environment and the potentially adversely impacted First Nation, develop and implement a First Nations consultation plan, and directly notify First Nations at existing public notice points. Alberta assumed that First Nations will take initiative in raising concerns and that project proponents will identify strategies to avoid, mitigate, or accommodate adversely affecting First Nations rights and traditional uses.

First Nations take issue with the Crown taking such a "hands-off" approach to consultation. Proponents are self-interest and driven by profit motives with no constitutional obligation to protect Aboriginal and treaty rights. The honour of the Crown may be met if the Crown consults with First Nations and get their approval of the consultation process to be engaged in with third parties before any consultation with industry begins, and if the Crown maintains a supervisory role ensuring that consultation between third parties and First Nations are conducted according to the plan approved by First Nations. In this way industry would be charged with the responsibility for the technical aspects including full disclosure, environmental assessments, etc., and the Crown would maintain responsibility for meeting procedural requirements.

Alberta's unwritten policy, directed by budgetary concerns, is to require First Nations to establish one-point consultation mechanisms for consultation with the province and the project proponent. At the province's initiative, First Nations established Industry Relations Corporations (IRCs) and Alberta has been providing funding for their operation. IRC shareholders are typically band members and the CEO is often a member of the community. The staff of IRCs includes an environmental coordinator who reviews environmental assessments and an Elders' coordinator who acts as a liaison between industry and the Elders and community members for consultation purposes. Rather than consulting with the community, industry proponents contact the First Nation's IRC and conduct all consultations through the corporation. In theory IRCs facilitate communication between First Nations and industry, but the CEO and directors of the IRCs are not usually politically accountable to the community and may not accurately reflect the views of the community, and thus the legitimacy of conducting consultation through IRCs is questionable.

After being notified of a development, First Nations must, according to the Guidelines, submit a valid statement of concern within the legislated submission period. These concerns must relate to the issues within the Director's authority and must relate directly to the proposed project. The person or entity filing the statement of concern must be directly affected by the activity.

This raises the concern of the capacity of First Nations to respond efficiently and effectively to protect their rights in the context of Alberta's overheated and rapidly developing economy. The province of Alberta and some industry proponents are actively negotiating with First Nations in various parts of the province to simultaneously create certainty for industry and enhance the capacity of First Nations to participate in consultation. The financial and technical demands placed on First Nations to consult have overwhelmed many small communities. The lack of capacity to answer the demands of consultation portends a situation in which First Nations are vulnerable to being steamrolled by project proponents, particularly considering the time constraints created by the Guidelines.

The Guidelines outline additional steps to the authorization process under the *Water Act.* The guidelines apply, at the discretion of the Director, to large scale water diversion, wastewater, or water works projects and projects off-reserve that may have a potential to adversely impact First Nations rights and traditional uses on reserves.[86] Upon being provided with project specific information by the project proponent, Alberta Environment will assess whether the project requires First Nations consultation and, if so, will advise potentially adversely impacted First Nations of the proposed project and regulatory timeline.[87] The project proponent will then be charged with the responsibility to develop a First Nations consultation plan to the satisfaction of the Director. Consultation may include advertisements in First Nations newspapers, community postings, face-to-face meetings with elected leaders or their delegated representatives, or any other means to inform members of the First Nation about the proposed project.[88] The project proponent is required to document their consultation efforts and outcomes, proposals for avoidance or mitigation, or where no agreement can be reached, written reasons. Alberta Environment will then make a final determination as to whether or not consultation was adequate, and if not, delay or deny regulatory approval. This begs the question of whether, if the

---

[86] Alberta's First Nations Consultation Guidelines on Land Management and Resource Development, September 1, 2006, Part IV at 1, accessed on-line at http://www.aand.gov.ab.ca/AANDFlash/Files/Albertas_Consultation_Guidelines.pdf .

[87] This appears to contradict the Court in *Marshall* which rejected Ministerial discretion in protecting treaty rights and appears to offend the constitutional prohibition against unstructured discretionary administrative regime which risks infringing constitutional rights.

[88] *Consultation Guidelines, supra* note 84 at 3.

consultation process itself was adequate, the First Nation could oppose the project. Given Alberta Environment's history of almost never denying project approvals, it is unlikely that First Nations' opposition alone, without a Court decision, could stop a project from proceeding.

6. Consultation Under the *Water Act*
6.1 The Water for Life Strategy

Water use has come to the foreground as various user groups compete for the limited water resources of Southern Alberta, the most prominent being urban centres, the oil industry, and irrigation farmers, whose priority is determined in keeping with the first-in-time-first-in-right licencing regime. Alberta allocates water use by issuing water licences under the *Water Act*. Developed pursuant to the *Water Act*, Alberta's "Water for Life" strategy mandates a consultation process with stakeholders in the allocation of water resources. The Alberta government, while being aware that Treaty and Aboriginal rights to water exist, has chosen to side-step dealing squarely with Aboriginal and Treaty water rights. By failing to address Aboriginal and Treaty water rights in Alberta's water legislation and policies, the province has adopted an unstructured discretionary administrative regime which risks infringing Aboriginal and Treaty rights. It is clear from the chapters following that Treaty 7 First Nations have residual Aboriginal and treaty rights to water and thus have a right to be consulted whenever their Aboriginal and Treaty rights to water are impacted. Alberta's "Water for Life" consultation process deprives First Nations of their rightful role in the consultation process.

6.1.1 Alberta's Water Consultation Process

In drafting the "Water for Life" strategy, the Alberta government held public consultations in the spring of 2002. Responsibility for conducting consultations was contracted out to a consultant which conducted 15 community workshops, analysed 2,100 workbooks completed by individuals, and did a random telephone survey of 1,000 Albertans. One of the water policy workshops included 13 representatives from Aboriginal and Métis communities and was concluded within five hours.

In the spring of 2003, the Alberta government was to meet with stakeholders who attended the Minister's Forum on Water. Only eight of the "stakeholders" who participated were individuals from First Nations. First Nations' rights were not incorporated into Alberta's water policy. The Environmental Strategies Advisor who coordinated the consultation process was unaware of which First Nations organizations were invited to participate in reviewing the draft discussion paper which was published in April, 2003.[89] Alberta Environment relied on the Alberta Ministry of Aboriginal Affairs and Northern Development to consult with the stakeholder First Nations. The discussion papers were mailed out on April 11, 2003 and the deadline for input on Alberta's water policy was May 31, 2003. The speed at which the Water for Life policy was drafted and approved, combined with the minimal input by First Nations, casts a dark shadow of doubt as to whether First Nations were adequately consulted at this stage of the process.

Although it is clear that First Nations have constitutionally protected rights and interests, the "Water for Life" strategy is completely silent on Aboriginal and Treaty rights. Because of the extensive impact of water use on the exercise of First Nations Treaty rights and reserve economies, Alberta should have consulted First Nations in a manner consistent with the Crown's on-going Treaty relationship with First Nations, not merely as members of the public or even as "stakeholders." All relevant information ought to have been provided to Treaty 7 First Nations in a timely manner. They should have been consulted before or at the same time as the public. The cumulative impact of Alberta's water policy needs to be examined because it affects not only Treaty hunting and fishing rights, but also rights to self-government, inter-governmental relations and future economic development. First Nations involvement in monitoring the health of the watershed will be on-going and funding will be required so that there can be continuing meaningful consultation.

Because water resources often originate outside traditional territories, it would most convincingly be argued that a duty to consult with First Nations exists regarding the use of waters within the watershed of the rivers flowing through their traditional territories and reserves. For the Treaty 7 First Nations, this includes, at minimum, the rivers named in Treaty 7: the Bow River, South Saskatchewan River, Red Deer River, Maple Creek, Old Man River, and Crow's Creek, Milk River, and St. Mary's River. All of these rivers are located within the larger South Saskatchewan River Basin pictured in figure 2-2.

---

[89] Personal interview with Justin Tone, Alberta Environment, July, 2004.

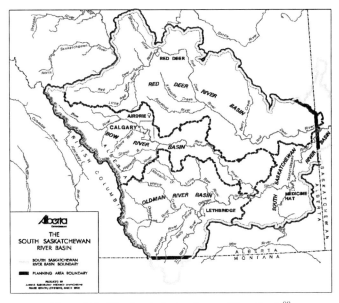

Figure 2-2. The South Saskatchewan River Basin[90]

6.1.2 Highlights of Alberta's Water Policy

Alberta's Water Policy adversely affects First Nations rights and interests in a number of significant ways, which gives rise to the duty to consult.

Alberta is committed to the principle of sustainable development. The Draft Discussion paper states that Alberta is committed to "sustainable development" by which is meant "development that meets the needs of the present without compromising the ability of future generations to meet their own needs." "Sustainable development" is a term of compromise. Encapsulated in this concept is the on-going tension between conservation and continuing development. Sustainable development will require input by First Nations and the participation by First Nations as partners in the decision-making process, particularly because development most impacts those people who live closest to the land, a point that is not acknowledged in the Water for Life strategy.

Alberta has taken a "watershed approach" to managing water resources. In the

---

[90] Map of the South Saskatchewan River Basin
http://www3.gov.ab.ca/env/water/regions/ssrb/Images/SSRB_large.jpg, accessed August 11, 2007.

"Water for Life" strategy, communities and stakeholders are responsible for watershed management and developing plans to ensure the supply and control the pollution of source water, including aquifers and groundwater. The province intends to develop a watershed source protection framework in collaboration with Watershed Advisory Councils, Watershed Protection Groups, municipalities and stakeholders. There is no mention of how First Nations will be involved in watershed management, if at all.

The watershed approach, if taken to its full extent, would mean that First Nations have a role to play in the management of virtually every body of water in Southern Alberta. The watershed approach, if First Nations are involved in a meaningful way, would be a great opportunity for Treaty 7 First Nations to promote their interests in water quality, quantity and flow because it extends past reserve and traditional territorial boundaries to source waters.

Alberta is undertaking plans to monitor and control drinking water quality. Quality drinking water is, of course, a necessity. It is not clear from the Water for Life strategy how Alberta would work with reserves to monitor and control drinking water quality. Roles and responsibilities need to be defined as reserves may be viewed by the province as federal jurisdiction. A cooperative approach that recognizes First Nations jurisdiction would be preferable, especially considering that pollutants potentially drain from outside First Nations lands into their drinking water resources. First Nations need to be involved in setting a consistent policy to be applied on and off-reserve. The issue of jurisdiction has come to the foreground in the conflict between the Town of Strathmore and the Siksika First Nation in a recent conflict over the EAB approvals of plans to dump the town's sewage upstream from the reserve.

The Provincial Water Advisory Council effectively deprives First Nations of their rights to self-government and jurisdiction over water resources. A provincial Water Advisory Council is made up of stakeholders and advises government, guides the implementation of the Water Strategy, and investigates and reports on existing and emerging water issues. While the Water for Life policy recognizes that the watershed approach to management ensures that those people who best understand and are immediately affected by water issues can help find solutions to address them, the province has made no commitment to reserving a role for First Nations on the Provincial Water Advisory Council. The province intended that First Nations would form committees or participate in volunteer community-based watershed protection groups.

The existing framework does not acknowledge Treaty rights and responsibilities and potentially divests First Nations of their jurisdiction over water resources by creating a "balancing of interests" process in which First Nations interests are superseded by those of powerful, well-funded stakeholders. The reason given by the province for not recognizing the unique position of First Nations is that watersheds transcend political, social and economic boundaries. This argument simply doesn't make sense considering federal jurisdiction in the areas of fisheries, navigation, national parks, and Indian reserves already overlaps with the province's general jurisdiction. Alberta's position was that involvement of stakeholders within each watershed would help Alberta succeed in improving water management. The province hoped that First Nations would participate in Watershed Advisory Councils that would have membership on the Provincial Water Advisory Council to share information, evaluate water issues and receive advice. A case in point is the Bow River Basin Council which is made up of representatives of a variety of stakeholders. The BRBC has made attempts to consult with First Nations, but only as one of many interest groups. To date the First Nations within the Bow River watershed, the Tsuu T'ina, Stoney and Siksika Nations play no active role in the BRBC.

The watershed approach may be an opportunity for First Nations to assert their right to water and their inherent jurisdiction to govern matters pertaining to reserve land. Through the use of trans-boundary agreements, First Nations may enhance their powers of governance. Alberta pays lip service to the idea of "shared governance" through a network of partnerships and collaboration between citizens, communities, industry and government. Alberta has made no clear commitments to "shared governance" or shared jurisdiction with First Nations. Classified merely as "stakeholders," First Nations are afforded the appropriate level of priority and their *sui generis* rights are not acknowledged. Rather, they are considered citizens as any other provincial resident without unique rights and responsibilities and without any specific jurisdiction over water resources.

Treaties and agreements govern the sharing of water between Canada and the United States, and between Alberta and B.C. and Saskatchewan. Alberta must receive a fair share of quality water from its upstream neighbours and, in turn, must pass on a fair share of quality water to its downstream neighbours. First Nations might consider establishing similar trans-boundary agreements that will ensure entire watersheds are managed appropriately. This approach may be most beneficial for the very large southern reserves of Treaty 7 First Nations.

The province considers healthy aquatic eco-systems for recreational use and does not seriously consider cultural, Aboriginal, or Treaty rights. Security of the right to hunting and fishing for future generations of First Nations requires healthy aquatic ecosystems. Alberta's Water for Life strategy calls for striking a balance between water used to support the economy and communities and water used to support healthy aquatic ecosystems. It is silent on how this balance will be attained and who will be consulted. The wording used suggests that the drafters have only considered the interests of recreational cottagers and sports hunters and fishermen and have not seriously considered hunting as a cultural, Aboriginal, or Treaty right. The very survival of First Nations cultures depends on healthy environments where cultural knowledge can be passed on to further generations.

Environmental assessments and consultation is only required for major water diversions, not for licenced use. Alberta Environment has allocated water licences and approvals for use by the oil and gas industry that is twice the amount of water used annually by the entire City of Calgary. It is worthy to consider whether the Treaty 7 Tribal Council ought to press for consultation on major water licences to industry, especially considering that most of the water used is turned saline and only recycled with great difficulty and expense.

Communities have become polarized over the issue of water management. The Town of Strathmore, having run out of space for its sewage, was granted temporary approval in February, 2007 to release its wastewater into the Bow River, just 15 kilometres upstream from the Siksika reserve. The town had been using six lagoons to store its sewage, but the latest population explosion led Strathmore to look for other options. The town built a 20 mile long pipeline at the cost of $10 million to discharge treated wastewater into the Bow River.

The central issue in the matter is whether the Siksika First Nation was adequately consulted prior to issuing the Approval. The Siksika Nation filed an application for judicial review on May 19, 2006. The judicial review was restricted to considering the sufficiency of consultation with the Siksika Nation by Alberta Environment prior to issuing the Approval. On September 6, 2006 Justice McIntyre dismissed the Judicial Review for being premature. The Siksika Nation appealed to the Court of Appeal stating that the duty to consult and accommodate is a duty that exists independently of the result of the appeal process. The duty to consult and accommodate cannot "be met or cured after the issuance of the approval." Furthermore, the appeal procedure set out under Part 4 of the *Environmental Protection and Enhancement Act* is not an adequate alternative remedy. Unfortunately for those of us with an interest in consultation law, the matter was adjourned and has not yet been heard.[91]

6.2   The South Saskatchewan River Basin Water Management Plan

Alberta Environment prepared the South Saskatchewan River Basin Water Management Plan and led the planning process. The consultation process was a combined effort by Alberta Environment, Alberta Agriculture, Food and Rural Development, and Alberta Sustainable Resource Development, and Fisheries and Oceans Canada. For the first five years of planning the SSRB consulted with four Basin Advisory Committees located in the Red Deer River, Bow River, Oldman River, and South Saskatchewan River sub-basins. First Nations were not actively involved in the consultation process for reasons that are unclear. Basin Advisory Committees, such as the Bow River Basin Council, maintain that they made efforts to include First Nations in the consultation process to no avail. Nevertheless, without First Nations involvement the Committees provided their recommendations leading to the drafting and approval of the South Saskatchewan River Basin Water Management Plan.

The province clearly takes the position that reserves do not include reserved water rights, and that Treaty water rights are not a priority right. The provincial position is that "while water development and licensing took place during the past century, First Nations in the SSRB were not in a position to obtain water licences with sufficient priority for a reliable water supply. With the exception of the Piikani [Peigan] Nation, water needs remain unresolved."[92] Alberta Environment claims to have consulted with potentially affected First Nations, but the extent of that consultation is not clear.[93]

---

[91] Environmental Appeals Board, "Status of Active Appeals" retrieved on-line April 6, 2007 from http://www.eab.gov.ab.ca/status.htm.

[92] Alberta Environment, "Background Information for public consultation on the South Saskatchewan River Basin Draft Water Management Plan" and "Approved Water Management Plan for the South Saskatchewan River Basin (Alberta)," August 2006 http://www3.gov.ab.ca/env/water/regions/ssrb/pdf/SSRB_Plan_Phase2.pdf , accessed on November 17, 2006.

[93] When the writer approached the individuals representing First Nations on the Basin Advisory Committees, their various legal counsel warned the writer and the individuals that discussion of consultation may prejudice negotiations.

7. Conclusion

Alberta's Consultation Guidelines and Water for Life strategy, may meet the province's requirements for consultation, but do not provide the mechanism for meaningful and substantial consultation, and most importantly, do not meet the constitutional standard of consistency. To a large extent Alberta has devolved its responsibility to consult with First Nations to project proponents. While there are opportunities for First Nations to be involved in watershed management planning through the watershed advisory councils, their involvement is not mandatory. The experience of developing the South Saskatchewan River Watershed Management Plan has shown that watershed management policies may be set without First Nations' participation. Even when they participate, they are only one of many "stakeholders" with no special acknowledgement given to their Treaty and Aboriginal rights to water.

In the writer's opinion, it appears that the fundamental problem stems from the starting point of consultation. First Nations will only be consulted if the project proponent and AENV determine that their large scale water diversion, wastewater, or water works projects and projects off-reserve that may have a potential to adversely impact First Nations rights and traditional uses on reserves. Upon such determination, responsibility for consultation is devolved to the project proponent with AENV taking monitoring consultation processes and results. The cumulative environmental effects of water use is best dealt with at the level of water management planning, a process in which Treaty 7 First Nations have not been involved. Post-project-proposal consultation, while necessary, is inadequate to address cumulative impacts or effects on the exercise of livelihood rights off-reserve.

CHAPTER THREE: RECONCILIATION AND CONSULTATION

1. Introduction

It has been argued that the current challenge is for Canada to achieve reconciliation with First Nations in a manner that refrains from assimilation and restores Aboriginal people to a meaningful place within the constitutional order, and reinforces a relationship marked by collaboration and partnership.[1] The Supreme Court has indicated that the aim of reconciliation is to balance Aboriginal and other interests.[2] Consultation is the most important means of achieving the overarching purpose of reconciliation.

In describing how consultation serves the purpose of reconciliation, McLachlin C.J. stated in *Haida* that consultation and accommodation are on-going processes of fair dealing extending from the time of assertion of sovereignty and continuing *beyond* formal claims resolution.[3] Reconciliation, then, is never concluded: it is an on-going relationship stemming from the Constitutional guarantee of Aboriginal rights, the assertion of Crown sovereignty over the lands and resources of Aboriginal peoples, and the honor of the Crown:

> Reconciliation is not a final legal remedy in the usual sense. Rather, it is a process flowing from rights guaranteed by s. 35(1) of the *Constitution Act, 1982*. This process of reconciliation flows from the Crown's duty of honourable dealing toward Aboriginal peoples, which arises in turn from the Crown's assertion of sovereignty over an Aboriginal people and *de facto* control of land and resources that were formerly in the control of that people. As stated in *Mitchell v. M.N.R.*, [2001] 1 S.C.R. 911, 2001 SCC 33, at para. 9, "[w]ith this assertion [sovereignty] arose an obligation to treat aboriginal peoples fairly and honourably, and to protect them from exploitation" (emphasis added).[4] Supreme Court decisions in the past 16 years have established that the central purpose of s.35(1) is reconciliation. Although the cases dealing with reconciliation vary in definition, statement of purpose, and description of process, one principle is clear: Negotiation and consultation with First Nations on issues of natural resource use are integral to the process of reconciliation. The central objective of reconciliation, as a cornerstone of the constitutional relationship of Aboriginal peoples with Canada, will

---

[1] Michael Hudson, "Reconciling Diversity with Unity: Canadian Federalism in the 21st Century" unpublished paper presented to the Canadian Bar Association Canadian Legal Conference in Vancouver, August 14-16, 2005.

[2] *R. v. Van der Peet*, [1996] S.C.J. No. 77, [1996] 2 S.C.R. 507 at para. 31 [*Van der Peet*]; *Delgamu'ukw v. British Columbia*, [1997] S.C.J. No. 108 (QL); [1997] 3 S.C.R. 1010 at para. 186 [*Delgamuuk*]; *Haida Nation v. British Columbia (Minister of Forests)*, [2004] 3 S.C.R. 511; [2004] S.C.J. No. 70 (Q.L.); 2004 SCC 73 at para. 14 [*Haida*].

[3] *Haida, supra* note 2 at para. 32.

[4] *Ibid.*

inform negotiations and consultations with regard to water rights and water resource management. The questions remaining are: what is reconciliation, what is to be reconciled, and how? To these questions, the Supreme Court has provided no consistent answers.

This chapter will analyze two political processes in Alberta employing negotiation and consultation and whether they meet the standard set by the Supreme Court for reconciliation and are consistent with s.35(1): 1) The Peigan Agreement that was negotiated between the Piikani (Peigan) First Nation, Alberta, and Canada and resulted in an agreement for the diversion of the Oldman River and use of the water for irrigation, and 2) Alberta's *Water Act* and Water for Life Strategy which sets out a process for on-going public participation in water management.

2. Reconciliation Evolving in Constitutional Law

Section 35(1) was incorporated into the Constitution in keeping with the constitutional principle of the protection of minorities.[5] Section 35(1) specifically protects the Aboriginal and Treaty rights of the Aboriginal peoples of Canada:

> 35(1) The existing aboriginal and treaty rights of the aboriginal peoples of Canada are hereby recognized and affirmed.

While the common law recognized the existence of Aboriginal rights, "[t]hrough the enactment of s.35(1), a 'pre-existing legal doctrine was elevated to constitutional status, or in other words, s.35(1) had achieved 'the constitutionalization of those rights.'"[6]

The *Sparrow*[7] case, decided by the Supreme Court of Canada in 1990, was the first in a long line of cases acknowledging the requirement of reconciliation under s.35(1) of the Constitution. Over the years the purpose and object of reconciliation has transformed from the reconciliation of federal power with federal duty (as in *Sparrow*), to the reconciliation of Aboriginal societies with the broader political community (as in *Delgamu'ukw*). The discussion below describes the characterization of reconciliation in the case law as it has evolved since 1990.

---

[5] *Reference re Secession of Quebec*, [1998] S.C.J. No. 61 (QL); [1998] 2 S.C.R. 217.

[6] *Van der Peet, supra* note 2 at para. 23; *Delgamuukw, supra note* 2 at para. 134.

[7] R. v. *Sparrow*, [1990] 1 S.C.R. 1075; [1990] S.C.J. No. 49 [*Sparrow*].

2.1 *Sparrow*: Federal Power to be Reconciled with Federal Duty

In *Sparrow*, the Supreme Court held that, while federal legislative powers continue, including the right to legislate with respect to Indians pursuant to s. 91(24) of the *Constitution Act, 1867*, they must be read together with s. 35(1) which provides protection of Aboriginal and Treaty rights. The *Sparrow* decision established that, although s.35(1) did not explicitly authorize the courts to assess the legitimacy of any government legislation restricting Aboriginal rights, the words "recognition and affirmation," restrained the exercise of sovereign power. The Court held that federal power must be reconciled with the federal duty to act in a fiduciary capacity with respect to Aboriginal peoples. The best way to reconcile federal legislative power with federal duty to Aboriginal peoples was to require justification of government regulation that infringes or denies Aboriginal rights. The reasons given for requiring reconciliation of federal powers with federal duties through the process of justification were the principle of liberal interpretation and the honour of the Crown:

> Such scrutiny is in keeping with the liberal interpretive principle enunciated in *Nowegijick, supra*, and the concept of holding the Crown to a high standard of honourable dealing with respect to the aboriginal peoples of Canada as suggested by *Guerin v. The Queen, supra*.[8]

2.2 *Van der Peet*: Reconciling Prior Occupation with Crown Sovereignty and Reconciling Aboriginal Legal Perspectives and British Legal Perspectives

By 1996, the Supreme Court of Canada had refined its interpretation of the purpose of s.35(1) to reconcile the "pre-existence of distinctive aboriginal societies with the assertion of Crown sovereignty."[9] The Court determined that s.35(1) "provide[s] the constitutional framework through which the fact that aboriginals lived on the land in distinctive societies, with their own practices, traditions and culture, is acknowledged and reconciled with the sovereignty of the Crown."[10] Reconciliation is the foremost guiding principle behind the definition of s.35(1) Aboriginal rights.

---

[8] *Sparrow, supra* note 7 at para. 62.

[9] *Van der Peet, supra* note 2 at para. 49.

[10] *Ibid.* at para. 31.

In *Sparrow*, the Court recognized that it was "crucial to be sensitive to the aboriginal perspective itself on the meaning of the rights at stake," and, likewise, in *Van der Peet*, the Court determined that, "[i]n assessing a claim for the existence of an aboriginal right, a court must take into account the perspective of the aboriginal people claiming the right..."[11] In *Van der Peet*, the Court added the requirement that Aboriginal perspectives be framed in guise of Canadian law:

> The definition of an aboriginal right must, if it is truly to reconcile the prior occupation of Canadian territory by aboriginal peoples with the assertion of Crown sovereignty over that territory, take into account the aboriginal perspective, yet do so in terms which are cognizable to the non-aboriginal legal system.[12]

It could certainly be argued that this is a nearly impossible task because of the great difference between the individual-based property-and-commodity-oriented British legal system and the communal-based natural laws of Aboriginal peoples. Madame Justice McLachlin, in her dissent in *Van der Peet*, characterized reconciliation differently. She shed some light on the purpose of s.35(1), stating that the desire for reconciliation of these two vastly different legal systems was the impetus behind the adoption of s.35(1) protection for Aboriginal and Treaty rights:

> [T]he essence of aboriginal rights is their bridging of aboriginal and non-aboriginal cultures: '...there will always be a question about which legal culture is to provide the vantage point from which rights are to be defined...a morally and politically defensible conception of aboriginal rights will incorporate both legal perspectives.'[13]

The Supreme Court majority characterized the central purpose of reconciliation as balancing and incorporating the legal *perspectives*, but not the actual *laws* or *legal systems*, of the colonizer and the colonized:

> [T]he only fair and just reconciliation is, as Walters suggests, one which takes into account the aboriginal perspective while at the same time taking into account the perspective of the common law. True reconciliation will, equally, place weight on each.[14]

Madame Justice McLachlin's dissent is examined in more depth below.

---

[11] *Ibid.* at para. 49.

[12] *Ibid.*

[13] *Ibid.*

[14] *Ibid.* at para. 50.

2.3 *Gladstone* and *Delgamu'ukw*: Reconciliation of Aboriginal Societies with the Broader Political Community

Chief Justice Lamer, in *Gladstone* and *Delgamu'ukw*, following the reasoning in *Van der Peet*, stated that one of the purposes underlying the recognition and affirmation of aboriginal rights by s.35(1) is the "reconciliation of aboriginal prior occupation with the assertion of the sovereignty of the Crown."[15] He further explained that at the stage of justification, the purpose of reconciliation shifts from the reconciliation of the prior occupation of Aboriginal people with the assertion of Crown sovereignty to the reconciliation of Aboriginal societies with the broader political community:

> some limitation of those rights will be justifiable. *Aboriginal rights are a necessary part of the reconciliation of aboriginal societies with the broader political community* of which they are part; limits placed on those rights are, where the objectives furthered by those limits are of sufficient importance to the broader community as a whole, equally a necessary part of that reconciliation.[16] (emphasis mine)

Lamer C. J.'s analysis appears to shift from incorporating different legal perspectives to implementing a balancing-of-interests legal analysis. It appears that this characterization of the reconciliation process compromises the protection of Aboriginal rights and operates at cross-purposes with the very essence of s.35(1). Lamer C. J. justifies placing limitations on Aboriginal rights, explaining that it is a necessary aspect of reconciliation, as in the case of conservation legislation. Goals that are consistent with the reconciliation of Aboriginal societies with the larger Canadian society are compelling and substantial objectives justifying limitations on Aboriginal rights:

> Because conservation is of such overwhelming importance to Canadian society as a whole, including aboriginal members of that society, it is a goal the pursuit of which is consistent with the reconciliation of aboriginal societies with the larger Canadian society of which they are a part. In this way, conservation can be said to be a compelling and substantial objective which, provided the rest of the Sparrow justification standard is met, will justify governmental infringement of aboriginal rights.[17]

After the goal of conservation is met, Lamer C. J. suggests that the distribution of resources be guided by:

---

[15] *Delgamuukw, supra* note 2 at para. 161; *R. v. Gladstone*, [1996] 2 S.C.R. 723; [1996] S.C.J. No. 79 (QL) at para. 73 [*Gladstone*].

[16] *Delgamuukw*, ibid.; *Gladstone*, ibid..

[17] *Gladstone*, ibid.

objectives such as the pursuit of economic and regional fairness, and the recognition of the historical reliance upon, and participation in, the fishery by non-aboriginal groups...In the right circumstances, such objectives are in the interest of all Canadians and, more importantly, the reconciliation of aboriginal societies with the rest of Canadian society may well depend on their successful attainment.[18]

The process of reconciliation thus evolved from placing equal emphasis on Aboriginal and non-Aboriginal legal perspectives to the pursuit of economic and regional fairness and recognition of the historical reliance upon the resources by non-Aboriginals. The Court explained the link between reconciliation of prior existing Aboriginal societies with asserted Crown sovereignty to the balancing-of-interests analysis, stating that "distinctive aboriginal societies exist within, and are part of, a broader social, political and economic community."[19]

The Supreme Court, applying this dictum in *Gladstone* to the Treaty context, stated that "[t]his observation applies with particular force to a treaty right." Where a Treaty contemplates the sharing of resources, and the Treaty right may be exercised on a commercial scale, the Court will take into account the fact that First Nations "constitute only one group of participants, and regard for the interest of the non-Natives...may be shown in the right circumstances to be entirely legitimate." In applying this principle to the treaty context, the balancing of interests analysis will consider the proportionality of the use of the resource.[20]

2.4 Madame Justice Mclachlin's Alternative View of Reconciliation

The threat of assimilation was the motivation of Aboriginal people for pressing for protection of Aboriginal and Treaty rights. The characterization of the process of reconciliation as an exercise of balancing of interests appears to weaken the protection of s.35(1) and expose Aboriginal and Treaty rights to erosion beyond recognition and meaningfulness. In Lamer C.J.'s conception of reconciliation, limitations on Aboriginal rights are a necessary part of reconciliation. The task is to determine which goals are indeed consistent with reconciliation and, furthermore, to decide who is charged with determining that these are compelling and substantial objectives. The Court admits that, at the justification stage, "[t]he range of legislative

---

[18] *Ibid.* at para. 75.

[19] *Delgamuukw, supra* note 2 at para. 165.

[20] *R. v. Marshall (II)*, [1999] 4 C.N.L.R. 301 at para 42 [*Marshall*].

objectives that can justify the infringement of aboriginal title is fairly broad."[21] This range of legislative objectives that fulfill the purpose of reconciliation includes

> the development of agriculture, forestry, mining, and hydroelectric power...general economic development...protection of the environment or endangered species, the building of infrastructure and the settlement of foreign populations to support those aims...[22]

It is hard to conceive of any resource-based Aboriginal right that would not be affected by this analysis. The balancing-of-interests form of "reconciliation" could potentially erode Aboriginal rights to the point where there is very little of substance left.

Madame Justice McLachlin did not agree with this approach. In her view: "...the framers of section 35(1) deliberately chose not to subordinate the exercise of Aboriginal rights to the good of society as a whole."[23] Legislative objectives that would satisfy the criteria for a justified infringement of Aboriginal rights ought be confined to those that seek to ensure the responsible exercise of the right, such as conservation or the prevention of harm to others. Legislative objectives that would negate or diminish the right itself could not be justified.

Madame Justice Mclachlin objected to Chief Justice Lamer's approach on the basis that it is:

> indeterminate and ultimately may speak more to the politically expedient than to legal entitlement...governments may abridge aboriginal rights on the basis of an undetermined variety of consideration. While "account" must be taken of the native interest and the Crown's fiduciary obligation, one is left uncertain as to what degree. At the broadest reach, whatever the government of the day deems necessary in order to reconcile aboriginal and non-aboriginal interests might pass muster...upon challenge in the courts, the focus will predictably be on the social justifiability of the measure rather than the rights guaranteed.[24]

In her view Lamer C.J.'s analysis "falls short of the 'solid constitutional base upon which subsequent negotiations can take place.'"[25] Agreeing that "reconciliation between aboriginal and non-aboriginal communities [is] a goal of fundamental importance," she was of the view that in

---

[21] *Delgamuukw, supra* note 2 at para 165.

[22] *Ibid.*

[23] *Van der Peet, supra* note 2 at para. 308.

[24] *Ibid.* at para. 309.

[25] *Ibid.*; *Sparrow, supra* note 7 at p.1105.

working to achieve this goal, it was unnecessary to depart from the principle of justification as elaborated in *Sparrow*:

> one of the two fundamental purposes of s.35(1) was the achievement of a just and lasting settlement of aboriginal claims...such a settlement must be founded on reconciliation of aboriginal rights with the larger non-aboriginal culture in which they must, of necessity, find their exercise. It is common ground that '...a morally and politically defensible conception of aboriginal rights will incorporate both [the] legal perspectives' of the 'two vastly dissimilar legal culture' of the European and aboriginal cultures'...The question is how this reconciliation of the different legal cultures of aboriginal and non-aboriginal peoples is to be accomplished. More particularly, does the goal of reconciliation of aboriginal and non-aboriginal interests require that we permit the Crown to require a judicially authorized transfer of the aboriginal right to non-aboriginals without the consent of the aboriginal people, without treaty, and without compensation? I cannot think that it does.[26]

Where Lamer C.J. conceives of a broad range of legislative objectives that would justify infringement of Aboriginal rights and title, McLachlin J. warns of the danger of unrestrained infringements in the name of "reconciliation." McLachlin J. alludes to reconciliation through a process of treaty-making requiring consent and compensation. It appears altogether reasonable that reconciliation between pre-existing Aboriginal societies and the assertion of Crown sovereignty take the form of treaty-making in the modern context, particularly in situations where First Nations have a well-developed legal tradition governing relationships through treaty, as is the case in the Treaty 7 territory.

Section 35 is the promise to Aboriginal Canadians of recognition of their rights. Lamer C.J. has stated that fulfillment of the promise of Aboriginal rights protection is achieved through negotiation, with the ultimate purpose of reconciling Aboriginal interests with those of the larger society. It is not surprising that First Nations are uneasy with this type of "protection" that mandates the discussion of their rights in a broad political forum, with the only safeguard being the vague notion of the "honour of the Crown," however powerful that concept may be in a legal context. "Section 35 represents a promise of rights recognition, and '[i]t is always assumed that the Crown intends to fulfill its promises. This promise is realized and sovereignty claims reconciled through the process of honourable negotiation..."[27]

---

[26] *Van der Peet, ibid.* at para. 310.
[27] *Haida, supra* note 2 at para. 20.

Section 35 protects the integral and defining features of distinctive Aboriginal cultures even if such features did not receive legal recognition and approval from European colonizers.[28] The underlying purpose of s.35(1) is the reconciliation of the pre-existence of aboriginal societies with the sovereignty of the Crown. The means to achieving reconciliation is settlement by Treaty or agreement, negotiated in good faith, and reinforced by the judgments of the Court.

> Treaties serve to reconcile pre-existing Aboriginal sovereignty with assumed Crown sovereignty, and to define Aboriginal rights guaranteed by section 35 of the *Constitution Act, 1982*.[29]

Reconciliation, in keeping with s.35 and the honour of the Crown, will lead to just and enduring settlement of Aboriginal claims:

> ...section 35 recognizes not only prior aboriginal occupation, but also a prior legal regime giving rise to aboriginal rights which persist, absent extinguishment. And it seeks not only to reconcile these claims with European settlement and sovereignty but also to reconcile them in a way that provides the basis for a just and lasting settlement of aboriginal claims consistent with the high standard which the law imposes on the Crown in its dealings with aboriginal peoples.[30]

In *Marshall* and *Bernard* the Court grappled with devising a process for reconciling Aboriginal and Crown perspectives on the law. The first step requires the court to examine the nature and extent of the Aboriginal practice prior to the assertion of Crown sovereignty, then to seek the corresponding common law right to determine the nature and extent of the modern right.[31]

In *Marshall* and *Bernard*, Mclachlin J. explained the role of the Aboriginal perspective as being more than assisting "in the interpretation of Aboriginal practices in order to assess whether they conform to common law concepts of title."[32] She recognized that Aboriginal laws themselves provide the Aboriginal perspective on the occupation of their land. "The relevant laws

---

[28] *R. v. Coté*, [1996] S.C.J. No. 93; [1996] 3 S.C.R. 139; 138 D.L.R. (4th) 385; 202 N.R. 161; 110 C.C.C. (3d) 122; [1996] 4 C.N.L.R. 26; 65 A.C.W.S. (3d) 760; 32 W.C.B. (2d) 96 at para. 52.

[29] *Delgamuukw, supra* note 2 at para. 186.

[30] *Van der Peet, supra* note 2 at para. 230.

[31] *R. v. Marshall; R. v. Bernard*, [2005] S.C.J. No. 44; 2005 SCC 43; [2005] 2 S.C.R. 220; 255 D.L.R. (4th) 1; [2005] 3 C.N.L.R. 214; 2005 CarswellNS 317 at para. 51 [*Marshall & Bernard*].

[32] *Ibid.* at para. 130, quoting J. Borrows, "Creating an Indigenous Legal Community" (2005), 50 *McGill L.J.* 153, at p. 173.

consisted of elements of the practices, customs and traditions of Aboriginal peoples and might include a land tenure system or laws governing land use."[33]

Quoting John Borrows, McLachlin J. acknowledged that Aboriginal law is more than mere evidence of occupation and land use:

> Aboriginal law should not just be received as evidence that Aboriginal peoples did something in the past on a piece of land. It is more than evidence: *it is actually law*. And so, there should be some way to bring to the decision-making process those laws that arise from the standards of the indigenous people before the court.[34] (emphasis added)

True reconciliation requires taking into account Aboriginal laws and perspectives. Mclachlin J. expanded on this approach in *Marshall* and *Bernard* when she explained that "[t]aking the Aboriginal perspective into account does not mean that a particular right, like title to the land, is established. The question is what modern right best corresponds to the pre-sovereignty Aboriginal practice, examined from the Aboriginal perspective."[35] She quoted the following observation of John Borrows:

> The idea is to reconcile indigenous and non-indigenous legal traditions by paying attention to the Aboriginal perspective on the meaning of the right at stake.[36]

Borrows explains that First Nations law and non-Aboriginal legal systems are not necessarily inconsistent. The "over-reliance on non-Aboriginal legal sources has resulted in very little protection for Indigenous peoples." He argues that the assertion of Crown sovereignty and the co-existence of British common law with First Nations law did not alter First Nations law, customs or conventions. "The suis generis doctrine reformulates similarity and difference and thereby captures the complex, overlapping, and exclusive identities and relationships of the parties."[37]

---

[33] *Marshall & Bernard, ibid.*

[34] *Ibid.* at para. 130.

[35] *Ibid.* at para. 52.

[36] Borrows, *supra* note 32 at para. 52.

[37] John Borrows, *Recovering Canada: The Resurgence of Indigenous Law*, (Toronto: University of Toronto Press, 2002).

2.5   *Haida*: Reconciliation as Balance and Compromise

Following the Supreme Court majority's opinions in *Van der Peet*,[38] and *Delgamuukw*,[39] the court advocated consultation, an exercise in balancing of interests, as a means of achieving reconciliation:

> [The] duty to consult and accommodate by its very nature entails balancing of Aboriginal and other interests and thus lies closer to the aim of reconciliation at the heart of Crown-Aboriginal relations...[40]

In *Haida* the Court once again emphasized the balancing of interests, this time characterizing the balancing act as between Aboriginal concerns with the potential impact on asserted rights and other societal interests:

> Balance and compromise are inherent in the notion of reconciliation. Where accommodation is required in making decisions that may adversely affect as yet unproven Aboriginal rights and title claims, the Crown must balance Aboriginal concerns reasonably with the potential impact of the decision on the asserted right or title and with other societal interests.[41]

3.   Checks and Balances on Consultation and Reconciliation

If reconciliation was to be merely a balancing of interests, clearly the protection of Aboriginal rights guaranteed by s.35(1) would be rendered meaningless and the supremacy of the constitution as dictated by s.52(1) would be merely a pipe dream. It is some consolation, therefore, that the Court acknowledges checks and balances on the process of reconciliation. In particular, consultation is to be guided by the principle of the honour of the Crown early in the claims process.

The basis for consultation as a means to reconciliation is "the principle of the honour of the Crown" which, the Court stated, "must be understood generously" as extending "from the assertion of sovereignty to the resolution of claims and the implementation of treaties. Nothing less is required if we are to achieve "the reconciliation of the pre-existence of aboriginal societies with the sovereignty of the Crown"[42]

---

[38] *Van der Peet, supra* note 2 at para. 31.

[39] *Delgamuukw, supra* note 2 at para. 186.

[40] *Haida, supra* note 2 at para. 14.

[41] *Ibid.* at para. 50.

[42] *Ibid.* at para. 17, *Delgamuukw, supra* note 2 at para. 186, quoting *Van der Peet, supra* note 2 at para. 31.

The potential rights embedded in these claims are protected by s. 35 of the *Constitution Act, 1982*. The honour of the Crown requires that these rights be determined, recognized and respected. This, in turn, requires the Crown, acting honourably, to participate in processes of negotiation. While this process continues, the honour of the Crown may require it to consult and, where indicated, accommodate Aboriginal interests.[43]

The honour of the Crown arises from the "Crown's assertion of sovereignty over an Aboriginal people and *de facto* control of land and resources that were formally in control of that people."[44] The Court noted that it is because First Nations were never conquered that reconciliation is required, and that one means to reconcile First Nations' claims with the sovereignty of the Crown is through negotiated treaties. With the assertion of sovereignty "arose an obligation to treat aboriginal peoples fairly and honourably, and to protect them from exploitation."[45]

Because the goal of reconciliation and the honour of the Crown go hand in hand, reconciliation and consultation are required at the early stages of claims resolution, even before there is proof of a valid claim to Aboriginal rights:

> To limit reconciliation to the post-proof sphere risks treating reconciliation as a distant legalistic goal, devoid of the "meaningful content" mandated by the "solemn commitment" made by the Crown in recognizing and affirming Aboriginal rights and title: *Sparrow, supra*, at p. 1108. It also risks unfortunate consequences. When the distant goal of proof is finally reached, the Aboriginal peoples may find their land and resources changed and denuded. This is not reconciliation. Nor is it honourable.[46]

In *Haida* the Supreme Court mandated consultation and accommodation even before final claims resolution "as an essential corollary to the honourable process of reconciliation that s. 35 demands." Consultation is required because it "preserves the Aboriginal interest pending claims resolution" and encourages the development of a relationship between the parties conducive to negotiations, which the Court state, is "the preferred process for achieving ultimate reconciliation." [47] The process of fair dealing and reconciliation "begins with the assertion of

---

[43] *Haida, ibid.* at para 25.

[44] *Ibid.* at para 32.

[45] *Ibid.* at para 32, quoting Mitchell v. M.N.R., [2001] 1 S.C.R. 911, 2001 SCC 33, at para 9.

[46] *Ibid.* at para 33.

[47] *Ibid.* at para 38; S. Lawrence and P. Macklem, "From Consultation to Reconciliation: Aboriginal Rights and the Crown's Duty to Consult" (2000), 79 *Can. Bar Rev.* 252, at p. 262.

sovereignty and continues beyond formal claims resolution." Reconciliation does not end with the resolution of Aboriginal claims.[48]

In *Haida*, an Aboriginal title case, the Court did not consider reconciliation and consultation post-Treaty: Maintaining the Treaty relationship as a means of reconciliation was considered in *Mikisew*.[49]

4. *Mikisew*: Reconciliation as "Managing" the Treaty Relationship

Where there is an existing treaty relationship, the Supreme Court has recognized that on-going consultation and reconciliation are inherent in that relationship. If reconciliation entails a process of reconciling the prior occupation of Aboriginal peoples with the assertion of Crown sovereignty in the political arena and resolving Aboriginal claims in keeping with the honour of the Crown, the most reasonable means of achieving that end is treaty-making or "managing" the existing treaty relationship. In *Mikisew*, the Supreme Court recognized that "unilateral Crown action (a sort of "this is surrendered land and we can do with it what we like" approach)…is the antithesis of reconciliation and mutual respect."[50] The Attorney General of Alberta denied that a duty of consultation can be an implied term of Treaty 8 because of the vastness of the Treaty 8 territory and the scattered settlement of First Nations. The Court rejected this argument and recognized that the Treaty 8 signatories "*did* in fact contemplate a difficult period of transition and sought to soften its impact as much as possible." The Court reiterated the "overarching objective of reconciliation rather than confrontation" as stated *Haida* and *Taku*.[51]

The *Mikisew* decision is significant because, where previous cases recognized that the fundamental objectives of reconciliation are to reconcile "aboriginal people and non-aboriginal peoples and their respective claims [and] interests," Mikisew added to those objectives the reconciliation of "ambitions." This definition of reconciliation broadened from reconciling pre-existing Aboriginal societies with the assertion of Crown sovereignty to reconciling Aboriginal societies with non-Aboriginal societies.

---

[48]   *Ibid.* at para 32.

[49]   *Mikisew Cree First Nation* v. *Canada (Minister of Canadian Heritage)*, [2005] S.C.J. No. 71 (QL); 2005 SCC 69.

[50]   *Ibid.* at para 49.

[51]   *Ibid.* at para 50.

This characterization of reconciliation is problematic for several reasons. It is the Crown that has an historical relationship with Aboriginal people, not all non-Aboriginal people (which includes by definition every immigrant new and old). It is the Crown that is held to a standard of fairness and honour. There is no standard to which all non-Aboriginal immigrant Canadians can be held in their dealings with Aboriginal peoples. Furthermore, the inclusion of interests and ambitions appears to open up Aboriginal territories to exploitation by new immigrants with new interests and new ambitions irrespective of the Crown's historical relationship. This new characterization of "reconciliation" could override the Treaties, particularly if equal weight is not given to Aboriginal legal traditions, Treaties and the common law.

5. Does Reconciliation Require Limitations on Aboriginal Rights?

While Lamer C.J. reasoned in *Gladstone* that the *Sparrow* test required expansion because of the lack of inherent limits on the aboriginal right to commercial fishing, Mclachlin J. suggested that Aboriginal rights are inherently limited by Aboriginal laws and customs and thus it is unnecessary to impose limitations by expanding the test of justification beyond what is required for conservation purposes. In her view, "[t]here is no need to impose further limits on it to affect reconciliation between aboriginal and non-aboriginal peoples."[52] Expansive limitations on Aboriginal rights in the name of "regional fairness" and economics go beyond what is required for reconciliation and threatens the very existence of Aboriginal rights:

> The extension of the concept of compelling objective to matters like economic and regional fairness and the interests of non-aboriginal fishers, by contrast, would negate the very aboriginal right to fish itself, on the ground that this is required for the reconciliation of aboriginal rights and other interests and the consequent good of the community as a whole. This is not limitation required for the responsible exercise of the right, but rather limitation on the basis of the economic demands of non-aboriginals. It is limitation of a different order than the conservation, harm prevention type of limitation sanctioned in *Sparrow*.[53]

McLachlin J. was also concerned that the test articulated by Lamer C.J. would leave Aboriginal rights vulnerable to abridgement by governments "on the basis of an undetermined variety of considerations" without setting the parameters for consideration of the Crown's fiduciary duty to protect the rights of Aboriginal peoples. Should government decisions be

---

[52] *Van der Peet, supra* note 2 at paras 301 and 312.
[53] *Ibid.* at para 306.

challenged in the Courts, in all likelihood, government decisions would stand, provide they met the test of "reasonableness." In her view, this is not adequate protection of Aboriginal rights:

> While "account" must be taken of the native interest and the Crown's fiduciary obligation, one is left uncertain as to what degree. At the broadest reach, whatever the government of the day deems necessary in order to reconcile aboriginal and non-aboriginal interests might pass muster. In narrower incarnations, the result will depend on doctrine yet to be determined. Upon challenge in the courts, the focus will predictably be on the social justifiability of the measure rather than the rights guaranteed. Courts may properly be expected, the Chief Justice suggests, not to be overly strict in their review; as under s. 1 of the Charter, the courts should not negate the government decision, so long as it represents a "reasonable" resolution of conflicting interests. This, with respect, falls short of the "solid constitutional base upon which subsequent negotiations can take place" of which Dickson C.J. and La Forest J. wrote in Sparrow, at p. 1105.[54]

Madam Justice McLachlin agreed with Lamer C.J. that reconciliation entails reconciling "aboriginal rights with the larger non-aboriginal culture in which they must, of necessity, find their exercise" but foresaw that the balancing-of-interests analysis articulated by Lamer C.J. would lead to the erosion of Aboriginal rights.

It is unnecessary to adopt the broad doctrine of justification because there are other means of "resolving" or "calibrating" the different legal perspectives of Aboriginal and non-Aboriginal people.[55] Given the internal limit of Aboriginal rights to natural resources, the task of reconciliation is then shifted to establishing the traditional right through the process of consultation and negotiation:

> As suggested in *Sparrow*, the government should establish what is required to meet what the aboriginal people traditionally by law and custom took from the river or sea, through consultation and negotiation with the aboriginal people.[56]

She recognizes that this may in fact be a relatively small percentage of the resource in question. Because Aboriginal societies did not value excess or accumulated wealth, "the measure will seldom, on the facts, be found to exceed the basics of food clothing and housing, supplemented by a few amenities." Beyond the "limited priority" for Aboriginal resource users, non-Aboriginal users "may enjoy the resource as they always have, subject to conservation."[57]

---

[54] *Ibid.* at para 309.
[55] *Ibid.* at para 313.
[56] *Ibid.* at para 311.
[57] *Ibid.* at para 311.

6.   How has Reconciliation Occurred to Date?

Development of water resources has required negotiations with Treaty 7 First Nations. Most recently the Peigan Water Use Agreement was concluded to allow the province to divert the waters of the Oldman River for irrigation. This Agreement is an example of the balancing-of-interests form of reconciliation. The results of the Agreement have yet to be seen, however there are rumblings of dissatisfaction with the Agreement within the constituents of the Piikani First Nation. The Water Act and Water for Life Strategy also employ a balancing-of-interests strategy in overall water management. Each will be considered in turn below.

6.1   The Peigan Water Use Agreement

The balancing-of-interests approach, rather than an Aboriginal rights approach, seems to have been taken in the 2001 Settlement Agreement concluded between Canada, the Piikani First Nation, and Alberta relating to use of water from the Oldman reservoir. The Piikani First Nation acknowledged "that Alberta operates the Reservoir to supply water throughout the Oldman River and the South Saskatchewan River basins." They furthermore agreed that during times of drought, Alberta would consult with all users in the Oldman River Basin, including the Piikani First Nation, and would "equitably distribute the stored water in the Reservoir to attempt to address the water needs of all such users along with the aquatic environment."[58]

Canada and Alberta signed the Peigan Agreement in order to discontinue litigation as to their respective rights, including ownership, entitlements or jurisdiction in relation to water from the Oldman River as it passes through the Piikani Reserve. Canada and Alberta apparently signed the agreement in recognition of the Piikani First Nation's interest in sharing the benefits derived from the water stored in the Oldman River Dam Reservoir without admitting that the Piikani First Nation has existing Treaty or Aboriginal rights to the waterbed of the Oldman River or to the water itself. That being said, Canada and Alberta agreed that the Agreement would not be taken to limit, diminish, or extinguish existing Aboriginal or treaty rights "except to the extent necessary to allow the implementation and continuation" of the Agreement.

All parties recognized "that it is in their best interests to resolve issues dealt with in this Agreement through negotiation or mediation." Like any negotiated settlement, there was clearly accommodation by all parties. The Piikani First Nation did not get explicit recognition of their

---

[58]   *Peigan Agreement*, 2001 at para 15.1.

Treaty and Aboriginal rights to the Oldman River. They agreed to discontinue their actions wherein they claimed Aboriginal and Treaty rights and interests to the riverbed and waters of the Oldman River and agreed to release Canada and Alberta from any such claims during the time in which the Agreement was in force. They abandoned their claims in exchange for a settlement package that included monies that would be, in part, invested in the Atco Power Limited hydro-electric project and irrigation project on the reserve. They also reserved for themselves, above and beyond water for household use and domestic livestock grazing:

> reasonable quantities of water for their on-reserve use from the Oldman River in order to meet the current and future needs of the Peigan for agricultural, irrigation, commercial, industrial or such other contemporary and traditional uses necessary for the health, economy environment and well-being of the Peigan people.[59]

For the purpose of the agreement, the parties agreed that this would amount to 35,000 acre feet per year. If this quantity is not enough, at the request of the Piikani First Nation, Alberta will enter into negotiations to increase the quantity allotted.

Furthermore it was agreed that a Follow-up Environmental Impact Assessment on the effects of the Reservoir on the reserve would be completed and that the parties would continue, by co-operative effort, to evaluate how the Piikani First Nation and the Oldman River valley are affected by the reservoir. Consultation will take place on an annual basis to report use of the Piikani First Nation's usage of the water. In addition, a representative of the Piikani First Nation will sit on the public advisory committee for the Water Management Review of the South Saskatchewan River Basin.[60]

The Peigan Agreement appears to be the type of negotiated settlement envisioned by Mr. Justice Lamer in so far as it balances the interests of all parties and provides the Piikani First Nation with a share of the benefit of water-related projected in the Oldman River Valley. The Agreement appears to do so without compromising the Aboriginal and Treaty rights of the Piikani First Nation, at least not explicitly. However, it remains to be seen how the terms of the Agreement play out 'on the ground.' It would not be surprising if the Piikani First Nation became concerned about lack of consultation in decisions regarding up-stream water use. While an allowance has been made to have one individual from the Piikani First Nation sitting on the public advisory committee for the Water Management Review of the South Saskatchewan River

---

[59] *Peigan Agreement* para 10.1.
[60] *Peigan Agreement* para 13.

Basin, it is conceivable that this minor role will not be viewed as adequate in the years ahead. The Piikani First Nation may have to rely on the evolving common law with regard to consultation to assert their on-going involvement in decisions relating to water management off-reserve that may affect their interests. It is conceivable that additional water management agreements will be required to enable the Piikani First Nation to play a more active role in decision-making regarding water use off-reserve that may affect water resources on reserve, particularly as Alberta Environment considers rerouting water from one river to another to serve urban centres and licence transfers from irrigation districts to municipalities.

6.2 Alberta's *Water Act* and Water for Life Strategy

Alberta's *Water Act* and Water for Life Strategy appears to provide an opportunity for reconciliation, however it is characterized. However, First Nations have not been meaningfully consulted on establishing either Alberta's Water for Life policy or its consultation guideline policy. Meaningful and substantial consultation must begin with consultation on the policies that establish the framework for water management. Not having done that, the province's Water for Life Strategy is a house built on the sand: having failed to acknowledge and protect Aboriginal and treaty rights and adhere to the principle of constitutionalism, the Water for Life Strategy does not have a firm foundation.

The Government of Alberta, led by Alberta Environment, has established a network of partnerships that it views as integral to achieving stewardship of water resources. The Government of Alberta will maintain partnerships with Provincial Water Advisory Councils, Watershed Planning and Advisory Councils, and Watershed Stewardship Groups. Alberta remains accountable and will continue to oversee water and watershed management activities in the province while working with these partners in planning.

Of the three "partners in planning," watershed planning and advisory councils (WPACs) have potentially the most significant role in managing Alberta's water resources, and in directly influencing policy and legislation development, tracking and reporting on the condition of watersheds and influencing change within watersheds. WPACs are established to involve communities and stakeholders in watershed management. WPACs are intended to lead in watershed planning, develop best management practices, foster stewardship activities within the watershed, report on the state of the watershed, and educate users of the water resource.[61]

One such WPAC in the Treaty 7 area is the Bow River Basin Council (BRBC) peopled by volunteers representing "stakeholders" including municipal governments, industry, environmentalists, recreational users, and First Nations. Any interested individual or organization can join the Bow River Basin Council. The BRBC is the advisory body that has developed a water management plan affecting the traditional territories of the Stoney, Tsuu T'ina, and Siksika Nations. First Nations are not currently represented on the Council despite the fact that very important decisions are being debated and decided that affect the entire watershed.

The reason for the lack of participation of First Nations on the BRBC is not apparent. There is a willingness on behalf of other stakeholders to involve First Nations in watershed planning, and indeed numerous participants recognize Treaty 7 First Nations' special constitutional protection. It appears that First Nations are immobilized by the fear that any participation on the Council will be construed as "consultation" and may somehow diminish their ability to claim Treaty water rights should they be compromised. Or perhaps, there is no faith in a voluntary, consensus-based process within a group that is over-populated by representatives from non-Aboriginal municipalities and industries. Furthermore, it appears that the two groups are simply not communicating about either the procedural or the substantive issues surrounding their potential participation in on-going water management issues. Members of the Bow River Basin Council have made efforts to engage their First Nations' neighbours at the community level with the understanding that participation with Water Policy and Advisory Councils does not replace the government's duty to consult.

Most importantly, First Nations take the position that they are not obligated to participate in watershed management planning at the WPAC level: They maintain that their relationship is with the Crown and any negotiations that take place should occur at the government-to-government level. There is some merit to this argument, as the treaty relationship is between the Crown and First Nations and the duty to consult cannot be devolved to third parties. However, there is nothing to stop First Nations from participating in all levels of decision-making at once, except the fear their participation might be somehow construed as consultation. This could be

---

[61] "Water for Life: Alberta's Strategy for Sustainability" accessed at http://www.waterforlife.gov.ab.ca/docs/strategyNov03.pdf on August 8, 2007.

remedied by putting consultation agreements and waivers in place at the outset to clarify the purpose of specific negotiations.

In my view it is time for First Nations to take initiative be actively participating in the formation of WPACs. WPAC's are an opportunity to engage in negotiations as recommended by the Supreme Court as a process for reconciling competing interests. First Nations' participation in the watershed planning process would ensure that they have the opportunity to have their views taken into consideration. Most importantly, <u>WPACs represent an opportunity to assert jurisdiction and share governance of the watershed in a way that reconciles Aboriginal interests, legal systems, and cultures with the assertion of Crown sovereignty and other competing interests.</u>

In Alberta's view, the purpose of consultation is to facilitate reconciliation of First Nations rights and traditional uses (not including rights arising from unextinguished proprietary rights) with land and resources development activities.[62] Involvement in WPACs goes way beyond consultation as it is currently defined by Alberta and industry. In practice, First Nations are only notified and consulted when a specific development is contemplated by a proponent within the Nation's traditional territory. Watershed planning is very much broader than that and requires proactive strategic planning and management. A WPAC has the power to create a Watershed Management Plan which, when approved by Alberta, is the standard by which all future proposals for development are to be measured. Involvement on WPACs would put First Nations in the drivers seat. Until now, First Nations have been side-lined: Proponents have posted notices in newspapers, paid a few dollars to some Elders, and gone on to complete their projects with very little input from local communities. This process of minimal consultation has led some community leaders to tender allegations of genocide.

WPACs could and should be inclusive of Treaty 7 First Nations, acknowledging that reconciliation is mandated by s.35(1) and Treaty 7 and affirming the special constitutional status of First Nations: First Nations are not merely stakeholders with a vague interest in water management. WPACs could be formed recognizing that the Treaty "provides a framework

---

[62] Alberta Environment, First Nation Consultation Guidelines (Regulatory Authorizations and Environmental Impact Assessments), Draft 1, May 18, 2006 at 2.

within which to manage the continuing changes in land use already foreseen [at the time of signing] and expected, even now, to continue well into the future."[63]

7. Conclusion

The overarching purpose of s.35(1) is reconciliation. It is clear from reviewing the case law, that there is no consistent characterization of the process of reconciliation. The definition of reconciliation ranges from reconciling pre-existing Aboriginal societies with the assertion of Crown sovereignty to reconciling Aboriginal societies with non-Aboriginal societies, to reconciling Aboriginal and non-Aboriginal rights, interests, and ambitions.

The characterization of reconciliation as a balancing of societal interests with Aboriginal interests is problematic because it circumvents the Crown's historical relationship with Aboriginal people. Only the Crown can be held to a standard of fairness and honour. There is no standard to which all non-Aboriginal immigrant Canadians can be held in their dealings with Aboriginal peoples. By including interests and ambitions in the balancing of interests process, Aboriginal peoples are at risk of being exploited due to competing societal interests and ambitions, including industrial interests and ambitions, irrespective of the Crown's historical relationship with Treaty 7 First Nations. This characterization of reconciliation would constitute a breach of the treaty relationship, particularly if equal weight is not given to Aboriginal legal traditions, treaties and the common law.

The objective of the Peigan Agreement was to balance the interests of all parties, the Piikani First Nation, Alberta, and Canada. Under this Agreement, the Piikani First Nation receives a share of the benefit of water-related projects in the Oldman River Valley. The Agreement does not preclude the Piikani First Nation from playing a participating in shared governance of water resources off-reserve.

The Water for Life Strategy created by Alberta in accordance with the province's *Water Act* creates an opportunity for Treaty 7 First Nations to participate in watershed governance through WPACs. However, in order for shared governance to be actualized, Treaty 7 First Nations' meaningful involvement in WPACs must be mandatory and WPACs must acknowledge the unique constitutional position of Treaty 7 First Nations. Acknowledgement and affirmation of Treaty 7 First Nations' s.35 rights would affect the constitution of the membership of WPACs

---

[63] *Mikisew, supra* note 49 at para 63.

as well as watershed management plans. Unless or until the special relationship between the Crown and Treaty 7 First Nations is recognized by WPACs, Alberta's Water for Life Strategy will not and cannot fulfill the goal of reconciliation.

Reconciliation may be achieved through negotiations between Treaty 7 First Nations and the Crown, guided by the principles of the Crown's honour, the duty of fairness, and constitutionalism. Adherence to these principles would protect Aboriginal peoples from exploitation. Where there is an existing treaty relationship, the Supreme Court has recognized that on-going consultation and reconciliation are inherent in that relationship.

There is no uniform standard for reconciliation: While Chief Justice Lamer recommends a balancing-of-interests approach to reconciliation, Madame Justice Mclachlin's analysis is closer to the heart of the purpose of s.35. The process of reconciliation must not subordinate Aboriginal and Treaty rights to societal interests: Reconciliation is best achieved by on-going Treaty negotiations. True reconciliation requires taking into account Aboriginal laws and perspectives. It may be argued that Treaty 7, being a pre-confederation treaty allowing the Crown to assert sovereignty throughout Blackfoot Confederacy territory, is also a constitutional document. Thus, any negotiations with Treaty 7 First Nations in the name of reconciliation, including consultation, must be consistent with the terms of Treaty 7.

The government should, through the process of consultation and accommodation, strive to establish "what is required to meet what the aboriginal people traditionally by law and custom took from the river or sea."[64] Expansive limitations on Aboriginal rights in the name of "regional fairness" and economics go beyond what is required for reconciliation, threaten the very existence of Aboriginal rights, and violate the principle of constitutionalism.

The fundamental issue for consultation with Treaty 7 First Nations is the establishment of a process for deciding water management policies. The question that must be answered through consultation with Treaty 7 First Nations is how Treaty 7 First Nations will be consulted in a meaningful and substantial way that is consistent with the principle of constitutionalism and the protection of their s.35 rights. This begs the question of whether Treaty 7 First Nations have sufficient rights to water to require consultation. The depth of consultation required depends on the nature and scope of their rights to water. The following chapters examines whether Aboriginal and Treaty water rights have been extinguished by the assertion of Crown

---

[64] *Van der Peet, supra* note 2 at para 311.

sovereignty, by treaty, and by the *NRTA* and legislation. If Treaty 7 First Nations' water rights have survived, consultation is required whenever the Crown contemplates conduct that might adversely affect those rights.

The Treaty relationship between Treaty 7 First Nations and the Crown provides the framework within which consultation and negotiation can take place. In my view, anything short of shared governance of the watershed is a breach of Treaty 7 water rights. Only through shared governance can Treaty 7 First Nations' interests, legal systems, and cultures be reconciled with the assertion of Crown sovereignty and other competing interests. Shared governance implies a level playing field in which Treaty 7 First Nations are not merely "stakeholders" whose interests in water resources can easily be ignored or minimized by more powerful and wealthy stakeholders such as Irrigation Districts and urban municipalities. Shared governance further implies recognition of the special constitutional place of Treaty 7 First Nations and respect for the treaty relationship between the Crown and Treaty 7 First Nations.

CHAPTER FOUR: ABORIGINAL RIGHTS AND TITLE TO WATER

1. Introduction

The principles of constitutionalism and the rule of law require all provincial government laws and actions to comply with the constitution: Government policies and decisions regarding consultation with Treaty 7 First Nations must be consistent with s.35(1) protection of Aboriginal and treaty rights. Whether or not the Crown is required to consult and the nature and scope the consultation required depends on whether there is a prima facie case for Aboriginal rights and title, and the nature and scope of those rights. To make out a prima facie case, First Nations must not only prove that they once possessed Aboriginal rights and title, but also that their Aboriginal rights and title have not somehow been extinguished.

This chapter identifies the tests for proving Aboriginal rights and title and applies these tests to Aboriginal rights and title to water as they existed prior to any treaties, historic acts by the Crown or legislation.

Subsequent chapters examine whether these original Aboriginal rights and title were extinguished, altered, or protected by treaty, and whether, after entering treaty, this bundle of rights was extinguished by Crown policy or Crown action, or by legislation. Only after existing Aboriginal rights and title to water are identified can we determine whether they are afforded protection under s.35(1) giving rise to a duty to consult prior to the province considering any action that may adversely effect those rights.

2. The Test for Identifying Aboriginal Rights protected by Section 35(1)

Aboriginal rights existed and were recognized under the common law. They were not created by s. 35(1) but subsequent to s. 35(1) they cannot be extinguished. They can, however, be regulated or infringed if such regulation or infringement satisfies the justificatory test laid out in *R. v. Sparrow*, part of which is the requirement that there must have been meaningful and substantial consultation.

The onus of establishing a prima facie infringement of an aboriginal right rests with the claimant: The first step is to identify the precise nature of the claim.[1] In *Van der Peet*, Lamer

---

[1] *R. v. Sappier*, 2006 SCC 54, J.E. 2006-2331, 50 R.P.R. (4th) 1, [2007] 1 C.N.L.R. 359, 274 D.L.R. (4th) 75, 355 N.R. 1, [2006] 2 S.C.R. 686, 214 C.C.C. (3d) 161, 799 A.P.R. 199, 309 N.B.R. (2d) 199, 2006 CarswellNB 676, per Bastarache.

est for identifying Aboriginal rights, emphasizing rights to participate in

> ...in order to be an aboriginal right an activity must be an element of a practice, custom or tradition integral to the distinctive culture of the aboriginal group claiming the right.[2]

Bastarache J. greatly simplified the test to prove the existence of Aboriginal rights dividing it into two steps: 1) Identifying the precise nature of the claim; and 2) Determining whether the practice, custom, or tradition was integral to the distinctive culture. Below, these steps will be applied to determine what Aboriginal water rights existed in the area covered by Treaty 7 prior to the signing of Treaty 7.

2.1 Step One: Identify the Precise Nature of the Claim

Justice Bastarache, writing for the Court, in *Sappier* redefined the *Van der Peet* test on "how to define the distinctive culture" of the Aboriginal groups and how to determine which pre-contact practices were integral to their distinctive culture. Echoing the supreme Court in *N.T.C. Smokehouse*[3], he stated that the key factors to consider in identifying the precise nature of the claims are "the nature of the action which the applicant is claiming was done pursuant to an aboriginal right, the nature of the governmental regulation, statute or action being impugned, and the practice, custom or tradition being relied upon to establish the right."[4]

The Court reiterated, in *Sappier*, that Aboriginal rights protect Aboriginal practices, customs and traditions, not Aboriginal rights to resources:

> Aboriginal rights are founded upon practices, customs, or traditions which were integral to the distinctive pre-contact culture of an aboriginal people. They are not generally founded upon the importance of a particular resource. In fact, an aboriginal right cannot be characterized as a right to a particular resource because to do so would be to treat it as akin to a common law property right.[5]

---

[2] *R. v. Van der Peet*, [1996] S.C.J. No. 77, [1996] 2 S.C.R. 507 at para 46. All references are to Lamer C.J. writing for the majority unless otherwise specified.

[3] *R. v. N.T.C. Smokehouse Ltd.*, [1996] 2 S.C.R. 672.

[4] *Sappier, supra* note 1 at para. 20, quoting *Van der Peet, supra* note 2 at para. 53

[5] *Ibid.* at para. 21.

That said, Bastarache J., referring to the *Adams*[6] decision, explained that the Supreme Court has recognized Aboriginal rights based on evidence showing the importance of the resource to pre-contact cultures. This begs the question of whether s.35 can only be used as a shield and defence when Aboriginal rights holders contravene legislation. Surely s.35 protection is meaningless if it cannot also be used as a sword to proactively protect Aboriginal rights by conserving the resources upon which Aboriginal rights holders rely. For example, the right to fish for subsistence on lakes and rivers within traditional territories is a meaningless if there are no fish or if the fish are contaminated and would pose a health risk if eaten. The promise of s.35 would be empty if the resource upon which Aboriginal people rely for their practices, customs, and traditions is destroyed.

The first step in identifying the precise nature of the claim is to grasp the importance of the resource to the Aboriginal group. In order to understand the importance of the resource, the Court "seeks to understand how that resource was harvested, extracted and utilized."

> The task of this Court is to define aboriginal rights in a manner which recognizes that aboriginal rights are rights but which does so without losing sight of the fact that they are rights held by aboriginal people because they are aboriginal. The Court must neither lose sight of the generalized constitutional status of what s. 35(1) protects, nor can it ignore the necessary specificity which comes from granting special constitutional protection to one part of Canadian society. The Court must define the scope of s. 35(1) in a way which captures both the aboriginal and the rights in aboriginal rights.[7]

The claimed right must relate to pre-contact culture or way of life of the Aboriginal group. The Court has required that the claimant prove that the practice, custom, or tradition was "integral to the distinctive culture" or the particular Aboriginal society. To pass this part of the test, the identified practice will ultimate "define the distinctive way of life of the community as an Aboriginal community."[8]

Accurately characterizing the pre-contact practice will influence considerations of how the practice "might have evolved to its present-day form."[9]

---

[6] *R. v. Adams*, [1996] 3 S.C.R. 101; 138 D.L.R. (4th) 657; 202 N.R. 89; 110 C.C.C. (3d) 97; [1996] 4 C.N.L.R. 1.

[7] *Sappier, supra* note 1 at para 22.

[8] *Ibid.*

[9] *Ibid.* at para 23.

In *Sappier* the Court explained that the characterization of resource use for personal uses was too general because such a characterization did not identify a practice that defined the way of life or distinctiveness of the Aboriginal community. By re-characterizing the right as a right to harvest wood for domestic uses for "such things as shelter, transportation, tools, and fuel" which are directly associated with the nomadic hunting and fishing lifestyle of the Mi'kmaq and Maliseet people, the right was specific enough to trigger s.35 protection.

2.2   Step two: Central significance of Practices, Customs, and Traditions

Identifying whether the tradition, practice or custom is an integral part of the distinctive culture of an Aboriginal community is important to the process of reconciliation and consultation.[10] The Supreme Court in *Van der Peet* had required that the practice, custom or tradition must be a "central and significant part of the society's distinctive culture" to qualify for s.35 protection. Certain things would not be considered distinctive. For example, qualities that are true of every human society (e.g., eating to survive), or "aspects of the aboriginal society that are only incidental or occasional to that society." [11] Aboriginal rights claimants were required to prove that a specific "practice, custom or tradition is a defining feature of the culture in question:"[12]

> To recognize and affirm the prior occupation of Canada by distinctive aboriginal societies it is to what makes those societies distinctive that the court must look in identifying aboriginal rights. <u>The court cannot look at those aspects of the aboriginal society that are true of every human society (e.g., eating to survive)</u>, nor can it look at those aspects of the aboriginal society that are only incidental or occasional to that society; the court must look instead to the defining and central attributes of the aboriginal society in question. It is only by focusing on the aspects of the aboriginal society that make that society distinctive that the definition of aboriginal rights will accomplish the purpose underlying s. 35(1) (emphasis mine).[13]

The statement of Lamer C.J. in *Van der Peet* had been interpreted to mean that Aboriginal practices required for survival could not be the subject of a claim to Aboriginal rights. Because every human society uses water for domestic purposes, the test as articulated in *Van der Peet*

---

[10]   *Van der Peet, supra* note 2 at para 31.
[11]   *Ibid.* at para 56.
[12]   *Ibid.* at para 59.
[13]   *Ibid.* at para. 56

would be an insurmountable barrier to prove Aboriginal rights to water, except for ceremonial purposes, such as the sundance, and possibly for watering horses.

Bastarache J. in *Sappier* reformulated the 'integral to a distinctive culture test':

> Although intended as a helpful description of the *Vanderpeet* test, the reference in *Mitchell* to a "core identity" may have unintentionally resulted in a heightened threshold for establishing an aboriginal right. For this reason, I think it necessary to discard the notion that the pre-contact practice upon which the right is based must go to the core of the society's identity, i.e. its single most important defining character. This has never been the test for establishing an aboriginal right. This Court has clearly held that a claimant need only show that the practice was integral to the aboriginal society's pre-contact distinctive culture.[14]

Bastarache J. explained Lamer C.J.'s reasoning, revealing that the pre-contact practice, custom or tradition relied need not be distinct; it need only be distinctive.[15] Barriers to recognizing Aboriginal rights were created by "[T]he notion that the pre-contact practice must be a "defining feature" of the aboriginal society, such that the culture would be "fundamentally altered" without it." Bastarache J. cautioned Courts to be wary of using this as the test of distinctiveness. 'Distinctiveness' is really about Aboriginal specificity: Aboriginal people were the original organized society occupying and using Canadian lands, therefore the focus of the Court should be

> on the nature of this prior occupation on the *nature* of this prior occupation. What is meant by "culture" is really an inquiry into the pre-contact way of life of a particular aboriginal community, including their means of survival, their socialization methods, their legal systems, and, potentially, their trading habits. The use of the word "distinctive" as a qualifier is meant to incorporate an element of aboriginal specificity. However, "distinctive" does not mean "distinct", and the notion of aboriginality must not be reduced to "racialized stereotypes of Aboriginal peoples" (J. Borrows and L. I. Rotman, "The *Sui Generis* Nature of Aboriginal Rights: Does it Make a Difference?" (1997), 36 *Alta. L. Rev. 9*, at p. 36).

In determining what is 'distinctive' the Court is urged to "seek to understand how the particular pre-contact practice relied upon related to that way of life."

Uses of resources may, in certain contexts meet the integral to a distinctive culture test even when it is for survival purposes:

> That the standard an aboriginal community must meet is distinctiveness, not distinctness, arises from the recognition in Sparrow, supra, of an aboriginal right to fish for food.

---

[14] *Sappier, supra* note 1 at para. 40.
[15] *Ibid.* at para. 36.

Certainly no aboriginal group in Canada could claim that its culture is "distinct" or unique in fishing for food; fishing for food is something done by many different cultures and societies around the world. What the Musqueam claimed in Sparrow, supra, was rather that it was fishing for food which, in part, made Musqueam culture what it is; fishing for food was characteristic of Musqueam culture and, therefore, a distinctive part of that culture. Since it was so it constituted an aboriginal right under s. 35(1).[16]

In *Sappier*, the Court rejected the argument that qualities common to every human society could to be protected as Aboriginal rights. Extending *Adams*[17] and *Coté*,[18] the Court stated the scope of s. 35 should extend to protect the means by which an aboriginal society traditionally sustained itself. The Court, referring to *R. v. Jones*, [1996] 2 S.C.R. 821 (S.C.C.), at para. 28; and *Mitchell*, at para. 12, explained that the *Van der Peet* test emphasizes practices that are vital to the life of the aboriginal society in question.

Applying this analysis to water rights would mean that Treaty 7 First Nations should be able to establish Aboriginal rights to water for transportation, for drinking and household purposes, and for raising horses. The rivers throughout their traditional territories were important trade routes throughout history. The use of horses became central to plains Indians culture as horses facilitated buffalo-hunting, warfare, and mobility.[19] Treaty 7 First Nations ought also to be able to demonstrate that access to and use of pure water in the natural environment is an aspect of their distinctive cultural practice of the Sundance and other ceremonies. Access to clean water was "vital to the life of the aboriginal society." However, the Court stated clearly that "there is no such thing as an aboriginal right to sustenance." We might draw the conclusion, then, that there is no Aboriginal right to water. The Court went on to state that "[T]he traditional *means* of sustenance, meaning the pre-contact practices relied upon for survival, can in some cases be considered integral to the distinctive culture of the particular aboriginal people." By extension, there may be pre-contact practices involving water use, such as household use, livestock watering, and ceremonial purposes that are protected as Aboriginal rights. The practice of

---

[16] *Van der Peet, supra* note 2 at para. 72.

[17] *Adams, supra* note 6.

[18] *R. v. Coté*, [1996] S.C.J. No. 93; [1996] 3 S.C.R. 139; 138 D.L.R. (4th) 385; 202 N.R. 161; [1996] 4 C.N.L.R. 26.

[19] A relatively 'recent' cultural adaptation, horse husbandry was introduced prior to European contact and by 1750 had extended throughout the American plains through a process of cultural diffusion.

domestic use of water is "directly related to the way of life of Treaty 7 First Nations."[20] The fact that water was used "for survival purposes [may be] sufficient...to meet the integral to a distinctive culture threshold."[21] The protection of the 'means' of water use may be rendered meaningless, particularly if the water is not of a quality to sustain traditional practices.

For example, the pre-contact lifestyle of Treaty 7 First Nations was to move from place to place for hunting and gathering depending on the availability of species according to the seasons. The ability to camp at specific sites throughout the semi-arid plains was determined by the availability of potable water drawn from rivers and streams for drinking, washing, tanning hides, watering horses, and other domestic purposes. One might argue that there is no Aboriginal right to the water itself, however, if the quantity, quality, and flow of water is compromised to the extent that Treaty 7 First Nations are no longer able to hunt, gather, or raise horses at specific sites, is this not a breach of their Aboriginal right traditional uses of water?

Bastarache J.'s reasoning appears to support this proposition:

> I can therefore find no jurisprudential authority to support the proposition that a practice undertaken merely for survival purposes cannot be considered integral to the distinctive culture of an aboriginal people. Rather, I find that the jurisprudence weighs in favour of protecting the traditional means of survival of an aboriginal community.[22]

2.2.1 Continuity of the Claimed Right with Pre-contact Practice

Where *Van der Peet* emphasized the necessity of proving that the nature of the practice giving rise to a claim to Aboriginal rights was distinctive of the particular cultural group, the new approach under *Sappier* emphasizes, the issue of how Aboriginal pre-contact practices are analogous to modern practices or are progenitors of modern processes. The pre-contact practice, "along with its associated uses...must be allowed to evolve."[23] The Court "has consistently held that ancestral rights may find modern form" and that 'existing aboriginal rights' must be interpreted flexibly so as to permit their evolution over time." In fact, "[i]f Aboriginal rights are not permitted to evolve and take modern forms, then they will become utterly useless."[24]

---

[20] *Sappier, supra* note 1 at para. 46.

[21] *Ibid.* at para. 46.

[22] *Ibid.* at para 38.

[23] *Ibid.* at para 48.

[24] *Ibid.* at para 49 referring *R.* v. *Sparrow*, [1990] 1 S.C.R. 1075; [1990] S.C.J. No. 49 at p.1093.

The Court must determine the nature of an Aboriginal right in contemporary circumstances by evaluating whether the claimed modern practice has logically evolved from the pre-contact activity and is analogous or equivalent to the pre-contact activity "carried on in a modern economy by modern means."[25]

2.2.2 Site-specific Rights

Aboriginal rights are not merely an incident of their ownership of the land as suggested in *Sikyea*.[26] Aboriginal title is actually a sub-category of Aboriginal rights. "Aboriginal rights arise from the prior occupation of land, but they also arise from the prior social organization and distinctive cultures of aboriginal peoples on that land."[27] The Aboriginal claimant's relationship to the land as well as "the practices, customs and traditions arising from the claimant's distinctive culture and society" are of relevance to the identification and definition of Aboriginal rights.[28] Aboriginal rights are not limited to "circumstances where an aboriginal group's relationship with the land is of a kind sufficient to establish title to the land."[29]

Aboriginal rights may be exercised on a specific site even though Aboriginal title cannot be proven.[30] If a site-specific right is established, this does not mean that it is exercisable anywhere because it is independent of aboriginal title: It continues to be a right exercisable "on the tract of land in question."[31]

The Supreme Court explained further in *Delgamu'ukw* that Aboriginal rights can be characterized as laying along a spectrum with respect to their degree of connection with the land. At one end of the spectrum are Aboriginal rights that are the practices, customs and traditions integral to distinctive cultures: At the other end of the spectrum is Aboriginal title. Somewhere in the middle are site-specific activities that are exercised in particular places and may be "intimately related to a particular piece of land" to which Aboriginal title cannot be proven. The

---

[25] McLachlin C.J. explained in *R. v. Bernard*, [2005] 2 S.C.R. 220, 2005 SCC 43 (S.C.C.), at para. 25

[26] *R. v. Sikyea* (1964), 43 D.L.R. (2d) 150 at 152 (N.W.T.C.A.); aff'd [1964] S.C.R. 642.

[27] *Van der Peet*, *supra* note 2 at para 74; refered to in *Delgamu'ukw v. British Columbia*, [1997] S.C.J. No. 108 (QL); [1997] 3 S.C.R. 1010 at para 141.

[28] *Van der Peet*, *supra* note 2 para 74.

[29] *R. v. Adams*, *supra* note 6.

[30] *Ibid.*.

[31] *Ibid.* at para 30. The site-specific requirement for Aboriginal hunting and fishing rights is also recognized in *R. v. Coté*, [1996] S.C.J. No. 93; [1996] 3 S.C.R. 139; 138 D.L.R. (4th) 385; 202 N.R. 161; [1996] 4 C.N.L.R. 26.

Court in *Adams* gave the example of nomadic cultures where people changed the location of their villages in accordance with the seasons and conditions.[32] Although they may be unable to prove title to their traditional territories they may be able to prove site-specific rights.

In *Saanichton Marina*, a pre-*Sparrow* case, the B.C. Court of Appeal dealt with the claim by a Band to a Treaty right to carry on a fishery at a specific location. The Court determined that

> [w]hile the right does not amount to a proprietary interest in the sea bed...it does protect the Indians against infringement of their right to carry on the fishery, as they have done for centuries.[33]

Thus, an Aboriginal practice, falling short of title, may nonetheless be protected, as long as it satisfies the "necessary geographical element."[34] The geographical component of aboriginal rights is necessary to both ground and limit the extent of territory over which there exist specific rights. The geographic limits of the Aboriginal rights of the Blackfoot confederacy are described as the body of Napi, extending throughout southwestern Alberta (see Figure 1 below).[35]

3. The Test for Establishing Aboriginal Title to the Waterbeds in Southern Alberta

Equal weight must be given to considerations of the British common law proprietary interests in land and Aboriginal legal systems and perspectives in determining whether an Aboriginal group occupied a territory sufficient to establish Aboriginal title.

Aboriginal title is one type of Aboriginal right. The test for proof of Aboriginal title is an adaptation of the test for Aboriginal rights, the purpose of which is "to reconcile the prior presence of aboriginal peoples in North America with the assertion of Crown sovereignty" by recognizing and affirming "both aspects of that prior presence – first, the occupation of land, and second, the prior social organization and distinctive cultures of aboriginal peoples on that land..."[36]

---

[32] *Ibid.*; *Delgamu'ukw*, *supra* note 27 at para 138.

[33] *Claxton* v. *Saanichton Marina Ltd.*, [1989] 3 C.N.L.R. 46.

[34] *Sappier*, *supra* note 1 at para 51.

[35] "Metaphysics in Blackfoot Stories, Places and Ways of Knowing" Powerpoint presentation presented at Traditional Land Use Conference, Nakota Lodge, Morley, Alberta, March 16, 2007 by Kerry Scott, Piikani Chief & Council. To determine the specific sites and Aboriginal practices, customs, and traditions at those sites would require considerable research and is beyond the scope of this thesis.

[36] *Delgamu'ukw*, *supra* note 27 at para 141.

In that respect, Aboriginal title is a *sui generis* or unique right in land. Aboriginal title is a particular kind of Aboriginal right in land conferring the right to use the land for a variety of activities, so long as these activities are not irreconcilable with the nature of Aboriginal attachment to the land.[37]

In *Delgamu'ukw,* the Court set the framework for establishing claims to Aboriginal title. The criteria to be satisfied in making out a claim for Aboriginal title are as follows:

i) the land must have been occupied prior to sovereignty;
ii) if present occupation is relied on as proof of occupation pre-sovereignty, there must be a continuity between present and pre-sovereignty occupation; and
iii) at sovereignty, that occupation must have been exclusive.[38]

In applying these criteria to Treaty 7 First Nations' title to their traditional territories, it is evident that they had Aboriginal title.

3.1 Occupation at the Time of Assertion of Sovereignty

Prior to British presence on the plains, the ancestors of Treaty 7 First Nations a territory extending from the Rocky Mountains in the West to the Cypress Hills in the East and Peace Point in the North to Wyoming in the South. Their laws and languages reflected their understanding of their relationship with the land. Indeed, the very names for the rivers that have survived colonization and translation are a testament to their relationship with the waters.

> The land that Napi gave the Blackfoot is marked out by his body. Because of this they understood their land to have special places of power and significance. These places were regarded as sacred in the sense that they required respect and human self discipline. A lot of these places were used and still are, where possible, as vision quest areas.[39]

The place names marking the land that was known as the territory of the Blackfoot Confederacy is shown below:

---

[37] *Ibid.* at para 111.

[38] *Delgamu'ukw, supra* note 27.

[39] F. David Peat, *Lighting the Seventh Fire: The Spiritual Ways, Healing, and Science of the Native American* (Secaucus, N.J.: Carol Publishing Group, 1994).

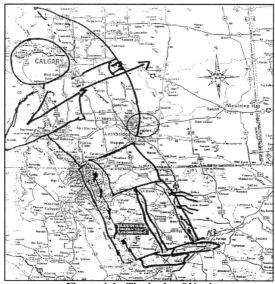

Figure 4-1. The body of Napi

This is the territory within which the Blackfoot followed the buffalo, their most important food source. Allied with one another, the Siksika, Kaini, Piikani, Tsuu T'ina, and Nakoda people defended their territories against the intrusion of the Cree and other tribes from the south.

3.1.1 Occupation...

To satisfy the first criteria, the occupation of the land claimed had to be more than an occasional presence. Aboriginal title exists only where the connection of the Aboriginal people to the particular piece of land on which the Aboriginal activities were taking place was of "central significance" to the distinctive culture of the group.[40] The Aboriginal group's "pattern of land holdings under aboriginal law" must be considered,[41] along with the use of land and the resources thereon. Aboriginal perspectives on occupation may be gleaned from traditional Aboriginal laws, including their system of land tenure or laws governing land use because those laws were elements of the practices, customs and traditions of aboriginal people. Furthermore, to determine whether occupation is sufficient to establish title, consideration must be given to "the

---

[40] *Adams, supra* note 6 at para 26.
[41] *Delgamu'ukw, supra* note 27 at para 147.

group's size, manner of life, material resources, and technological abilities, and the character of the lands claimed…"[42]

Lamer C. J. explained the connection between the occupation and the central significance of the particular piece of land:

> Occupancy is determined by reference to the activities that have taken place on the land and the uses to which the land has been put by the particular group. If lands are so occupied, there will exist a special bond between the group and the land in question such that the land will be part of the definition of the group's distinctive culture.[43]

Where occupation has been established and a substantial connection maintained, the central significance of the land to the claimant group's culture will be assumed, and need not be separately proven.[44]

The map of the Blackfoot Confederacy territory in figure 4-1 demonstrates the connection of Treaty 7 First Nations with the land. Depending almost exclusively on the buffalo hunt for their sustenance, they used the entire territory, following the buffalo herds as they migrated throughout the region.

Occupation the beds of waters or lands adjacent to streams and rivers might be established by the existence of structures such as fishing weirs, or by evidence that the watercourse was used for fishing,[45] hunting, or gathering aquatic plants. There is evidence that Treaty 7 First Nations had preferred areas along the river valleys which they claimed as their seasonal camping grounds. There were places along the river that were ideal for buffalo and other hunting, gathering medicines, grazing and watering their horses. It may also be possible to establish "occupation" of certain sites along rivers that were regularly used for travel, such as Blackfoot Crossing.

Occupation might also be proven by showing that other groups were prevented from using certain places. Historical records show that the Blackfoot Confederacy solidly defended their territories against intrusion. For example, they would only allow the Cree to hunt within their territories upon establishing treaties of peace. The explicit permission granted in Treaty 7 to

---

[42] *Ibid.* at para 149 quoting Kent McNeil, *Common Law Aboriginal Title* (Oxford: Clarendon Press, 1989) at pp. 201-2.

[43] *Delgamu'ukw, supra* note 27 at para 128.

[44] *Ibid.* at para 151.

[45] This is theoretical only, as the Blackfoot did not traditionally eat fish.

the Queen to travel on navigable streams lends credence to the idea that Treaty 7 First Nations occupied and controlled the waterways to the exclusion of others.

3.1.2 ...at the date of sovereignty

In *Delgamu'ukw*, the Court set the relevant date of inquiry for the assertion of Aboriginal title as "the time at which the Crown asserted sovereignty over the land subject to the title,"[46] whereas, the relevant date of inquiry for proof of Aboriginal rights has been set as the date of European contact. In the establishment of title, the date of the assertion of British sovereignty becomes key. The Canadian government takes the position that the date of assertion of British sovereignty was 1670, the year the Hudson's Bay Company was granted a charter over Rupertsland. This position is supported by two Federal Court cases, decided before *Delgamu'ukw*.[47] The government's alternate date for the assertion of British sovereignty is 1869, when Rupertsland was transferred to Canada. Both of these "assertions" of British sovereignty over the territory occurred without the knowledge of Treaty 7 First Nations who maintained their freedom to traverse borders and who governed their territories by a system of Treaties between the Siksika, Piikani, Kaini, Tsuu T'ina, and Nakoda peoples, protecting their territories from invasion from their enemies, principally the Cree, Sioux, and Shoshone. The assertion of British sovereignty only took on meaning with the presence of the RCMP sent by invitation of the Blackfoot confederacy to keep the destructive forces of the American whiskey trade out of Blackfoot territory. "Aboriginal title pre-dated colonization by the British and survived British claims of sovereignty."[48] The Blackfoot maintained their autonomy for more than 200 years after the Hudson's Bay Charter was granted and dominated the prairie without interference until the buffalo were decimated and the people were demoralized by the whiskey trade in the late 1800's. Arguably, if a similar burden of proof of actual occupation and not merely intention to occupy is imposed on the Crown, the date of sovereignty might be the date that there was a Northwest Mounted Police presence on the prairies, or the date of the Treaty. In any event, Treaty 7 is

---

[46] *Delgamu'ukw, supra* note 27 at para 142.

[47] *Hamlet of Baker Lake* v. *Minister of Indian Affairs and Northern Development (No.2),* [1980] 1 FMC 518 at 562; *Sawridge Band* v. *Canada,* [1995] 4 C.N.L.R. 121 at 143.

[48] *Roberts* v. *Canada,* [1989] 1 S.C.R. 322 at 340

evidence that the Crown recognized Aboriginal occupation of, and Aboriginal title to, what is now southern Alberta.

3.2 Continuity of Occupation

In *Delgamu'ukw* Lamer C.J. recognizes "conclusive evidence of pre-sovereignty occupation may be difficult to come by." In such cases

> an aboriginal community may provide evidence of present occupation as proof of pre-sovereignty occupation in support of a claim to aboriginal title. What is required, in addition, is a continuity between present and pre-sovereignty occupation, because the relevant time for the determination of aboriginal title is at the time before sovereignty.[49]

Continuity of occupation is a requirement to prove Aboriginal title, but there is "no need to establish 'an unbroken chain of continuity' between present and prior occupation." The Court recognized that occupation and land use "may have been disrupted for a time, perhaps as a result of the unwillingness of European colonizers to recognize aboriginal title." Too strict a requirement of continuity could undermine "the very purpose of s.35(1) by perpetuating the historical injustice suffered by aboriginal peoples at the lands of colonizers who failed to respect' aboriginal rights to land."[50]

Aboriginal title may exist despite a disruption in occupation, and despite a change in the "precise nature of occupation." If such is the case, it does not necessarily preclude a claim for aboriginal title, as long a substantial connection between the people and the land is maintained."[51]

Assuming Treaty 7 is a peace treaty and not a land cession treaty,[52] there is ample evidence of continuity of occupation of the waterbeds and waters in southern Alberta, although the "precise nature of the occupation" changed. When Treaty 7 First Nations were forced to give up the buffalo hunt, they made the transition to ranching and farming which required more intensive water use, especially for irrigation purposes.

---

[49]   *Delgamu'ukw, supra* note 27 at para 152.

[50]   *Ibid.* at para 153.

[51]   *Ibid.*

[52]   The distinction between peace treaties and land cession treaties is more fully dealt with in Chapter 4.

3.2.1 Internal Limits

The nature of the occupation is subject to internal limits, "i.e., uses which are inconsistent with continued use by future generations of aboriginals." Internal limits on uses of land flow from the special bond between Aboriginal peoples and the land claimed such that the land is part of the group's definition of themselves. In this type of situation, Aboriginal title lands cannot be used in a manner "irreconcilable with the nature of the occupation of that land and the relationship that the particular group has had with the land which together have given rise to aboriginal title in the first place." Because group's very identity depends on their relationship with the land, there is "an inherent limitation" on Aboriginal uses of land preventing them from using the land in a manner that would preclude them from using it for traditional purposes. [53]

This reasoning raises interesting questions, particularly for the Stoney and Piikani peoples. If a Treaty 7 First Nation could successfully prove title to a waterbed based on occupation for fishing and hunting purposes, would they forfeit their title by participating in a development project such as a hydro-electric dam resulting in the flooding of the lands and waters once used for fishing and hunting? If that is the case, governments and industrial developers can do what First Nations cannot without compromising their title, despite the pre-sovereignty continuous occupation of their traditional territories – participate in large-scale development projects that alter the use of the land and water.

3.3 Exclusive Occupation at the Time of Sovereignty

To prove Aboriginal title, Aboriginal people must show exclusive occupation, that is, the ability to exclude others from the lands held pursuant to that title. Proof of exclusivity should have regard to "the factual reality of occupation, as encountered by the Europeans" as well as the context of Aboriginal society at the time of sovereignty. If lands were used by "a number of bands, those shared lands would not be subject to a claim for aboriginal title, as they lack the crucial element of exclusivity."[54] But if other Aboriginal groups frequented the claimed lands and the Aboriginal group demonstrated their "intention and capacity to retain exclusive control,"[55] they may be able to prove exclusive possession.

---

[53] *Delgamu'ukw, supra* note 27 at para 154.
[54] *Ibid.* at para 159.
[55] *Ibid.*; McNeil, supra note 42 at 204.

Aboriginal laws and treaties may be evidence of exclusive occupation: "Aboriginal laws under which permission may be granted to other aboriginal groups to use or reside even temporarily on land would reinforce the finding of exclusive occupation."[56] Control over who is permitted to access Aboriginal lands is evidence of a group's exclusive control.[57] Exclusivity is evidenced by the intention and capacity to retain exclusive control.[58]

Treaty 7 appears to have officially granted the Queen and her subjects the right of navigation which was otherwise maintained as the exclusive right of Treaty 7 First Nations:

> ...reserving to Her Majesty, as may now or hereafter be required by Her for the use of Her Indian and other subjects, from all the Reserves hereinbefore described, the right to navigate the above mentioned rivers, to land and receive fuel cargoes on the shores and banks thereof, to build bridges and establish ferries thereon, to use the fords thereof and all the trails leading thereto...[59]

If more than one Aboriginal group occupied a particular territory, there may be shared exclusivity compatible with Aboriginal title so long as the right to exclude others was maintained. For shared exclusivity to exist, those that shared territory would have to be willing to share with each other to the exclusion of others. "There clearly may be cases in which two aboriginal nations lived on a particular piece of land and recognized each other's entitlement to that land but nobody else's."[60]

First Nations in southern Alberta had Treaty relationships with one another that protected their shared exclusive possession of certain tracts of land against encroachment by other enemy First Nations. First Nations in southern Alberta belonged to the Blackfoot Confederacy and together protected their lands from encroachment by the Cree and from First Nations south of the American border.[61]

It is clear that Treaty 7 First Nations satisfied the requirements for proof of Aboriginal title to the waters and waterbeds. Treaty 7 First Nations occupied southern Alberta prior to the

---

[56] *Ibid.* at para 157

[57] McNeil, *supra* note 42 at 204.

[58] *Delgamu'ukw, supra* note 27 at para 156; McNeil, *supra* note 42 at 204.

[59] Treaty No. 7, made 22nd Sept., 1877, between her Majesty the Queen and the Blackfeet and other Indian Tribes, at the Blackfoot Crossing of the Bow River, Fort Macleod (Ottawa: Queen's Printer and controller of Stationery, 1966).

[60] *Delgamu'ukw, supra* note 27 at para 158.

[61] See generally, Hugh Dempsey, *Crowfoot: Chief of the Blackfeet* (Halifax: Goodread Biographies, 1988).

assertion of sovereignty and the Crown recognized that occupation by entering into Treaty with them. Their occupation of the waters and waterbeds has been continuous, although the "precise nature of the occupation" changed following the disappearance of the buffalo and the settlement of Treaty 7 First Nations on reserves. Their occupation was exclusive, though shared, as is evidenced by the peace treaties by which the Blackfoot Confederacy was established and by their exclusion of other First Nations and the explicit clause in Treaty 7 limiting access to the rivers for travel purposes. If Treaty 7 did not extinguished Aboriginal title to the waters and waterbeds of southern Alberta, Treaty 7 First Nations may have a prima facie claim to Aboriginal title giving rise to the duty to consult regarding adverse affects to their waters.

4.   Conclusion

Prior to entering into treaty the Blackfoot Confederacy possessed a bundle of rights related to water including rights to navigation, rights to gather aquatic plants and medicines, rights to hunt, rights to assert jurisdiction, and rights to use water for all manner of domestic use and livelihood such as drinking, washing, tanning hides, and watering stock. These practices customs and traditions, related as they are to the Blackfoot Confederacy's pre-contact way of life, satisfy the test in *Sappier* that specific practices customs and traditions were integral to the distinctive culture.

Furthermore, Treaty 7 First Nations satisfied the requirements for proof of Aboriginal title to the waters and waterbeds. Treaty 7 First Nations occupied southern Alberta prior to the assertion of sovereignty and the Crown recognized that occupation by entering into Treaty with them. Their occupation of the waters and waterbeds has been continuous, although the "precise nature of the occupation" changed following the disappearance of the buffalo and the settlement of Treaty 7 First Nations on reserves. Their occupation was exclusive, though shared, as is evidenced by the peace treaties by which the Blackfoot Confederacy was established and by their exclusion of other First Nations and the explicit clause in Treaty 7 limiting access to the rivers for travel purposes.

Section 52 of the Constitution and the rule of law mandates that provincial government action, including consultation with First Nations, must be consistent with the protection of existing Aboriginal and treaty rights. The question to be answered is whether any Aboriginal rights or title survived Treaty 7 and subsequent legislation. If Treaty 7 did not extinguished

Aboriginal title to the waters and waterbeds of southern Alberta, Treaty 7 First Nations may have a prima facie claim to Aboriginal title giving rise to the duty to consult regarding adverse affects to their waters.

The Crown has the legal duty to consult and accommodate First Nation's rights and interests when it has knowledge, real or constructive, of the potential existence of the Aboriginal title and it contemplates conduct that might adversely affect Aboriginal title. To determine the scope of the Crown's duty to consult, it is necessary to make a preliminary assessment of the strength of the case supporting the existence of Aboriginal title to the waters and waterbeds of the rivers adjacent to their reserves and throughout their traditional territories, and the seriousness of the potentially adverse effect upon the right or title claimed.

The question remains whether their Aboriginal title to the waters and waterbeds extinguished by Treaty 7. Chapter 5 explores the meaning of Treaty 7 and the principles of Treaty interpretation in depth. For the purpose of this chapter, I will refer only to the text of the Treaty and will assume that it is possible for Aboriginal groups to assert title to the waterbeds and waters within their territories. Aboriginal title must be addressed separately from Aboriginal rights, even those that are intimately connected with land use.[62] If First Nations occupied a piece of land but did not do so exclusively, they might retain rights short of title, such as site specific rights.[63]

---

[62] *Adams, supra* note 6.

[63] *Delgamu'ukw*, supra note 27 at para 159.

CHAPTER FIVE: THE EFFECT OF TREATY 7 ON WATER RIGHTS

1. Introduction

The principle of constitutionalism and the rule of las demans that provincial regulation and action must be consistent with s.35 of the Constitution. Thus, provincial laws, regulations and policies relating to consultation must protect existing Aboriginal and treaty rights. Thus we must identify existing Aboriginal and treaty rights to determine whether Alberta's water and consultation policies are consistent with the protection of s.35 rights.

The preceding chapter we determined that Aboriginal rights and title existed prior to Treaty. Aboriginal rights, defined as the right to engage in practices, customs, and traditions within a specific territory included rights to navigation, rights to gather aquatic plants and medicines, rights to hunt, rights to assert jurisdiction, and rights to use water for all manner of domestic use and livelihood such as drinking, washing, tanning hides, and watering stock. Aboriginal title to water and waterbeds existed throughout the territory described by the Blackfoot Confederacy as the body of Napi, the Creator-being.

This Chapter examines whether Treaty 7 extinguished Aboriginal rights and title in whole or in part. Extinguishment of Aboriginal rights requires clear and plain intent of the Crown to do so and extinguishment of Aboriginal title can only be achieved when First Nations cede their title to the Crown, collectively, and willingly at a public meeting. If extinguishment is a term of the treaty, the principles of treaty interpretation require that there was a common intention of the Crown and First Nations parties to extinguish Aboriginal title and rights.

The question of whether Treaty 7 effectively extinguished Aboriginal rights or title can only be answered after ascertaining the purpose and intent of the treaty as understood by the First Nations and the Crown. The Supreme Court has established principles of treaty interpretation to assist in identifying the common intention of the parties. There is a distinct difference between the First Nations' view that the Treaty 7 was a peace treaty and the Crown's view that the treaty was a transfer of land. In the view of some Treaty 7 First Nations individuals, Aboriginal rights to hunt and Aboriginal rights to traditional territories were not extinguished: They claim Treaty 7 was a fraud. Treaty 7 First Nations had their own form of symbolic writing. When the Chiefs put their "X" on the Treaty, it did not mean that they accepted the terms of Treaty 7: The "X's" on the Treaty actually meant "full-stop" or a rejection of the Treaty.[1]

It is not unheard of for First Nations to press claims of Aboriginal title to waterbeds as well as the water itself, even after having entered into land cession Treaties. The Saugeen Ojibway Nation filed a Statement of Claim in the Ontario Superior Court of Justice,[2] claiming unextinguished Aboriginal title to the vast expanse of water and lakebed on Lake Huron and Georgian Bay in Ontario. The foundation of their claim is that the waters form part of the Saugeen Ojibway First Nation traditional territories. They had exclusively occupied their traditional territory at the time of the effective assertion of British sovereignty. Although they had entered into land cession treaties, the waters or waterbeds within their traditional territories had been specifically exempted from the land cession Treaties. Throughout the years following the Treaties, the Saugeen Ojibway Nation continued to assert their water rights. The waters of Lake Huron had supported the livelihood of the First Nations for thousands of years and the Saugeen Ojibway Nation had maintained exclusive possession of the territory. The people of Saugeen Ojibway Nation oppose a proposed $100 million pipeline to supply drinking water to Walkerton as well as the pipeline through Collingwood that supplies water to the Honda plant. The First Nation would now like to see the water taken from their unceded waters metered and paid for by the communities that use it.[3]

Similar to the Saugeen Ojibway Nation, the First Nations of the Treaty 7 may have an argument for unceded Aboriginal title to the waterbeds of the rivers flowing through their territories, despite the signing of Treaties. There is no question that the First Nations living in the Treaty 7 area had Aboriginal title to their territories, and with that title a right to the use of all waters within their territories.

This chapter will examine the meaning of the treaty by applying the principles of treaty interpretation, will consider whether the Treaty 7, as understood by the parties, extinguished

---

[1] This story was told to me by a member of the Piikani First Nation who did not want to be identified, and it was verified by several Nation members as being part of the oral history of the Piikani First Nation.

[2] Chippewas of Nawash Unceded First Nation and Saugeen First Nation v. The Attorney General of Canada, and Her Majesty the Queen in right of Ontario, Statement of Claim filed by John A. Othuis, Olthuis, Kleer, Townshend, December 23, 2003.

[3] Roberta Avery, Birchbark Writer, Owen Sound, February, 2004, "Band claims water rights" (http://www.ammsa.com/birchbark/topnews-Feb-2004.html#anchor1035625).

Aboriginal rights and title to water, and will suggest what, if any Aboriginal rights and title to water existed after Treaty 7.

2. **What is the Meaning of Treaty 7?**
2.1 **The Principles of Treaty Interpretation**

Treaties constitute a unique type of constitutional agreement. Attracting special principles of interpretation, they represent an exchange of solemn promises between the Crown and the various First nations. It is an agreement whose nature is sacred.

Treaty 7 First Nations have maintained from the date of signing that the treaty terms, agreed to orally, were binding both First Nations and the Crown and her representatives. However, English-Canadian jurisprudence has, until fairly recently, disregarded the oral history and oral terms of the Treaty, assuming that the only binding terms were written in the Treaty document. It is the position of Treaty 7 First Nations that the true terms of Treaty 7 include what was agreed orally by the parties and mutual promises made during negotiations, although Alberta takes exception to that proposition. Evidence of oral terms and promises may be gleaned from many sources, including the Commissioner's Report, witnesses' accounts, and oral history.

The goal of Treaty interpretation is to choose from among the various possible interpretations of common intention the one which best reconciles the interests of both parties at the time the Treaty was signed.[4] The examination of Treaty 7 negotiations below suggests that the interpretation of Treaty 7 that best reconciles the divergent interest of the parties is the view that Treaty 7 was meant to preserve peaceful co-existence and order on the western plains, and to ensure the livelihood of First Nations who faced annihilation along with the disappearing buffalo herds. There can be no reconciliation of the divergent views on the subject of the cession of Aboriginal title.

In order to assess and impute a common intention, one must examine the text, the historical context and evidence of the intentions and understanding of the parties, including oral histories. Because Treaties are a unique fusion of British common law and aboriginal customary law, the Court has suggested a number of principles of interpretation. A compilation of the

---

[4] *R. v. Sioui*, [1990] 3 C.N.L.R. 127.

principles of Treaty interpretation can be found in the two leading Supreme Court cases of *R. v. Marshall*[5] and *R. v. Badger*.[6]

The first stage in Treaty interpretation is to discover the common intention of the parties. In determining the signatories' respective understanding and intentions, the court must be sensitive to the unique cultural and linguistic differences between the parties. The words of the Treaty must be given the sense which they would naturally have held for the parties at the time: The words in the treaty must not be interpreted in their strict technical sense nor subjected to rigid modern rules of construction. Rather, they must be interpreted in the sense that they would naturally have been understood by the Indians at the time of the signing."[7] Ambiguities or doubtful expressions in the wording of the Treaty or document must be resolved in favour of the Indians. Any limitations which restrict the rights of Indians under Treaties must be narrowly construed. That being said, the terms of the Treaty cannot be altered "[w]hile construing the language generously... by exceeding what "is possible on the language" or realistic."

Treaty rights of Aboriginal peoples must not be interpreted in a static or rigid way. They are not frozen at the date of signature. The interpreting court must update Treaty rights to provide for their modern exercise. This involves determining what modern practice is an outgrowth of a core Treaty right.

In determining the common intention of the parties, the honour of the Crown is presumed, and is always at stake: It is always presumed that the Crown intends to fulfill its promises and no appearance of "sharp dealing" will be sanctioned. An extension of this principle is that Treaties will be interpreted in a manner which maintains the integrity of the Crown.

2.2   Historical Context of Treaty 7

Treaty 7 was negotiated and signed by the Siksika, Kainaiwa, Piikani, Tsuu T'ina, and Nakoda First Nations at Blackfoot Crossing in 1877. One of the greatest problems in negotiations was that no one individual present could speak all of the languages of the people present at Blackfoot Crossing.[8] The translation of the technical words might well have led to

---

[5]   *R. v. Marshall*, [1999] 4 C.N.L.R. 161; [1999] 3 S.C.R. 456; [1999] S.C.J. No. 55 (QL) at 199-200.

[6]   *R. v. Badger*, [1996] 1 S.C.R. 771; [1996] S.C.J. No. 39 (QL).

[7]   *R. v. Badger*, *supra* note 5 at para 52.

[8]   Treaty 7 Elders and Tribal Council et al., *The True Spirit and Original Intent of Treaty 7* (Montreal & Kingston: McGill-Queens University Press, 1996) at 124 [hereinafter Treaty 7 Elders].

different understandings. The Treaty 7 Elders say that Jerry Potts, interpreter for the Blackfoot, did not speak Blackfoot or English fluently and could not explain the meaning of "cede," "release," or "surrender."[9] The understanding left in the minds of the Blackfoot was that they were to share the surface of the land with the newcomers in return for being protected from outside incursion by the Queen's subjects.

Treaty 7 may be given several different interpretations. In the following discussion we will examine the meaning of the Treaty as a Peace Treaty and as a guarantee of continued hunting and economic development. If Treaty 7 is characterized as a peace Treaty, Treaty 7 First Nations may have residual jurisdiction, unextinguished Aboriginal title to natural resources including water within the ceded Treaty 7 territory. If the Treaty is a land cession Treaty, Treaty 7 First Nations may, nonetheless, possess residual jurisdiction and unceded title to the watercourses and water beds. At the very least they possess Treaty rights to beneficial use of, and shared jurisdiction over, water resources. In the proper circumstances "Aboriginal title and Treaty rights can co-exist in relation to the same land though the source of entitlement for each right is distinct."[10] In an effort to properly characterize and interpret Treaty 7 it is important to consider the historical context of Treaty negotiations.[11]

When a generous and liberal interpretation is made of the treaty in accordance with Blackfoot Confederacy understandings, it appears that the promise of continued hunting was a guarantee of the First Nation's signatories continued right and ability to hunt. However, First Nations freedom to hunt was limited by the treaty to land not taken up by settlement, mining, trading or other purposes. Waterways were not likely viewed by First Nations as lands capable of being "taken up" thus remaining unrestricted for hunting. First Nations retained rights to the

---

[9] Treaty 7 Elders, *supra* note 7 at 126.

[10] *R.* v. *Bernard*, [2003] 4 C.N.L.R. 48, N.B.C.A. per Daigle, J.A. rev'g *R.* v. *Bernard*, [2002] 3 C.N.L.R. 114 summary appeal court. The Appeal Court's decision was subsequently appealed to the Supreme Court of Canada as *R.* v. *Marshall*; *R.* v. *Bernard*, [2005] 3 C.N.L.R. 214 and was reversed on the basis that commercial logging is not a logical evolution of a Treaty or Aboriginal right.

[11] The court emphasized the importance of the historical facts in *R.* v. *Blais*, [2003] 2 S.C.R. 236; [2003] S.C.J. No. 44; 2003 SCC 44, a case that considered whether Metis were "Indians" for the purpose of s.13 of Manitoba's NRTA. While the Court focused on principles of constitutional interpretation, it emphasized the importance of analyzing the historical context to arrive at a correct interpretation. The success of an Aboriginal rights case clearly depends on the strength of the historical facts. Lawyers often fall prey to the notion that legal arguments and interpretations can establish Aboriginal rights. However, the Court has signaled to the profession that a more thorough historical analysis is required for future successes. This means doing the time-intensive, detailed work of sorting through archival haystacks to uncover historical needles, then piecing them together to find accurate meanings and interpretations.

rivers while the government reserved for itself the delegated right to navigate on certain rivers in the Treaty 7 Territory. Furthermore, First Nations chose their reserves, which were guaranteed to them in the written text of the treaty and oral promises, along the rivers to support hunting, their existing horse herds, cattle ranches and agriculture. It was not likely in the minds of either of the parties that huge dams would be built along the rivers and thus could not be "read in" as land taken up for "other purposes."

The Supreme Court recognized in *Badger* that the historical context as well as oral promises must be taken into account when interpreting the written text of the Treaties:

> [W]hen considering a treaty, a court must take into account the context in which the treaties were negotiated, concluded and committed to writing. The treaties, as written documents, recorded an agreement that had already been reached orally and they did not always record the full extent of the oral agreement.[12]

The Court recognized that there would be differences between the oral tradition and written Treaties: Treaties were drafted in English using specific legal language steeped in the tradition of British common law and had not been fully or accurately translated into the signatories' languages. Even if they had been, First Nations would likely have emphasized and remembered the oral promises because of their oral tradition.

> As a result, it is well settled that the words in the treaty must not be interpreted in their strict technical sense nor subjected to rigid modern rules of construction. Rather, they must be interpreted in the sense that they would naturally have been understood by the Indians at the time of the signing. This applies, as well, to those words in a treaty which impose a limitation on the right which has been granted.

To get a sense of the content of the Treaty right to water, it is essential to review the historical context of Treaty 7. Treaty 7 First Nations were by no means dependent on European trade prior to signing the Treaty. However, both Treaty 7 First Nations and the Hudson's Bay Company recognized that it was in their common interest to co-exist peacefully.[13] The Hudson's Bay Company recognized that the Prairie Indians were not dependent on trade goods and staples,

---

[12] *Badger, supra* note 5 at para 52.

[13] Revisionist fur trade historians have theorized that although First Nations were not hapless victims or the fur trade neither did they form "partnerships" with fur traders: They used their alliances with fur traders to their own advantages and maintained peaceful co-existence because it was mutually beneficial. Daniel Francis, Toby Morantz, *Partners in Furs: A History of the Fur Trade in Eastern James Bay, 1600-1870*, (McGill-Queen's University Press: 2003).

and to induce them to trade, they would have to encourage consumption of alcohol and tobacco.[14] By the time of Treaty signing the HBC had refrained from trading in alcohol and the Americans had taken up the trade.

By the 1870's the Blackfoot Confederacy had proven themselves to be a force to be reckoned with and dominated the plains of southern Alberta from the Cypress Hills in the East to the foothills of the Rockies and South to Montana and beyond. The land described by the Blackfoot as Napi's body[15] likely constituted their Aboriginal territory at the time of the assertion of British sovereignty. These First Nations had not been locked into debt service to the Hudson's Bay Company as their northern neighbors had been and were free of any need of the white man. They could obtain guns, ammunition, and horses through trade or spoil from the Americans. No need for the Queen's assistance arose until the buffalo, their main source of livelihood, had been depleted, and trading for American whiskey had so weakened their social fabric and physical strength that they required outside help.

By 1877, the year the Commissioners came to the Treaty 7 area, many of the First Nations of the Blackfoot Confederacy of southern Alberta were ready to enter into Treaty with the British. They hoped that by entering Treaty, they would be assured of the protection of the RCMP from their enemies and the assistance of the RCMP in driving out the whiskey traders that preyed on their susceptibility to alcohol and impoverished them in the trade of buffalo hides for whiskey. Oddly, Treaty 7 is silent on the prohibition of alcohol on reserves, which illustrates the lack of mutual understanding.

Chiefs whose Nations had not yet experienced the complete loss of the buffalo were opposed to signing the Treaty. Crowfoot, having mixed feelings of his own, recognized that the presence of the police was a boon to his people, but he was also aware of the risk that Treaty 7

---

[14] Simpson, in 1821 commented that he was "convinced that they must be ruled with a rod of iron, to bring and to keep them in a proper state of subordination, and the most certain way to effect this is by letting them feel their dependence upon us." While this was accomplished in the woodlands by locking Indian traders into debt service with the company, "[t]he plains Indians are a bold and independent race...and with them Tobacco and Spirits are the principle commodities; a Quart of Mixed Liquor will at time procure more Pounded Meat and Grease than a Bale of Cloth, indeed our whole profit in that Trade is upon those articles, and if Provisions were paid for in Dry Goods they would eat up all the gains of the Fur Trade." The debt system would not work, "as they can live independent of us, and by withholding ammunition, tobacco and spirits, the staple articles of the trade, for one year they will recover the use of their Bows and spear and lose sight of their smoking and Drinking habits; ...it will therefore be necessary to bring those Tribes round by mild and cautious measures which soon be effected." (Citation unavailable. Originally obtained from Dr. Frank Tough, Department of Native Studies, University of Saskatchewan, 1993.

[15] See Figure 4-1 on page 90 for the map.

First Nations might be losing their territories and natural resources. Speaking on behalf of all the Nations, Crowfoot accepted the terms of the Treaty as reported by Commissioner Laird:

> The plains are large and wide. We are the children of the plains, it is our home, and the buffalo has been our food always. I hope you look upon the Blackfeet, Bloods and Sarcees as your children now, and that you will be indulgent and charitable to them…The advice given me and my people has proved to be very good. If the Police had not come to the country, where would we all be now? Bad men and whiskey were killing us so fast that very few, indeed, of us would have been left today. The Police have protected us as the feathers of the bird protect it from the frosts of winter. I wish them all good, and trust that all our hearts will increase in goodness from this time forward. I am satisfied. I will sign the treaty."[16]

Despite his acceptance of the Treaty, Crowfoot's plea demonstrated his fears that the Treaty would result in great loss for Treaty 7 First Nations:

> Great Father! Take pity on me with regard to my country, with regard to the mountains, the hills and the valleys; with regard to the prairies, the forests and the waters; with regard to all the animals that inhabit them, and do not take them from myself and my children for ever. (emphasis mine)[17]

His impassioned plea, as recorded by Laird, was likely what prompted Lieutenant Governor David Laird's assurance that the Band's lands could not be taken without the consent of the Blackfoot people. Governor Laird made no mention of whether 'lands' included waters on the land. In his official report on treaty negotiations he explained:

> On Tuesday we met the Indians at the usual hour. We further explained the terms outlined to them yesterday, dwelling especially upon the fact that by the Canadian Law their reserves could not be taken from them, occupied or sold, without their consent.(emphasis mine)[18]

Lieutenant Colonel McLeod, Laird's co-Commissioner, reiterated this promise during the closing ceremonies:

> The Chiefs all here know what I said to them three years ago when the police first came to the country – that nothing would be taken away from them without their own consent. You all see today that what I told you was true…as surely as my past promises have been kept, so surely shall those made by the Commissioners be carried out in the future.

---

[16] Alexander Morris, *The Treaties of Canada with the Indians* (Toronto, 1880: reprint Toronto, Coles, 1971) at 272 (Hereinafter, Morris).

[17] Father C. Scollen to Lieutenant Colonel A. G. Irvine, April 13, 1879, No. 14924 in the Indian Affairs Archives, Ottawa, quoted in Hugh Dempsey, *Crowfoot: Chief of the Blackfeet* (Halifax: Goodread Biographies, 1988) at 105 (Hereinafter Dempsey).

[18] David Laird, Lieutenant Governor of the North-West Territories and Special Indian Commissioner, to unknown recipient, undated (ca October 1877) in Morris, *supra* note 15 at 257.

If they were broken I would be ashamed to meet you or look you in the face; but every promise will be solemnly fulfilled as certainly as the sun now shines down upon us from the heavens.[19]

Father Scollen, who attended Treaty signing, questioned whether Treaty 7 First Nations fully comprehended the legal significance of the Treaty. He believed that the signatories of the Treaty signed because they

> hoped that it simply meant to furnish them plenty of food and clothing, and particularly the former, every time they stood in need of them...Crowfoot, who, beyond a doubt, is considered the leading Chief of the Plains, did seem to have a faint notion of the meaning of the treaty...All the other Chiefs followed Crowfoot...[20]

It is evident from the historical record that Crowfoot had the understanding that the Treaty was a pact between Nations ensuring that, not only would the Red Coats continue to protect their territories, but that the Queen would come to their aid as the buffalo disappeared, in exchange for opening their land to white settlement.

2.2.1 Treaty 7 First Nations Understanding

Oral history indicates that all of the First Nations at Blackfoot Crossing in 1877 understood the Treaty to be a Treaty of Peace, putting an end to the whiskey trade and the heightened violence associated with alcohol consumption. Secondarily, it was a Treaty to share their land in return for economic assistance in the form of annuities.[21] The Blackfoot Confederacy understanding of Treaty 7 is that it conferred shared jurisdiction over land and water for mutual beneficial use:

> We believed and understood [that we would] share this territory amongst each other and we also believed that the land could not be given away because of its sacredness; therefore, it did not belong to us or anybody else. The earth is just put there by our creator for only our benefit and use.[22]

The Treaty 7 First Nations signatories certainly did not understand the treaty to be a cession of their rights to their traditional lands and waters as is illustrated by the peace and good order

---

[19] Address by James F. Macleod, Lieutenant Colonel, North-West Mounted Police, and Special Indian Commissioner, to the Indians of Treaty 7, September 21, 1877, in Morris, *supra* note 15 at 257.

[20] Father C. Scollen to Lieutenant Colonel A. G. Irvine, April 13, 1879, No. 14924 in the Indian Affairs Archives, Ottawa, quoted in Dempsey, *supra* note 16 at 106.

[21] Treaty 7 Elders, *supra* note 7 at 113.

[22] Louise Crop Eared Wolf, Blood, *Ibid.* at 114.

clause in the treaty. They interpreted the treaty as being an agreement to share the fruits of the land, but not the land itself. The concept of surrendering land was foreign to the Bloods who tell a story about Red Crow's offer to the Commissioners:

> At the signing of the treaty at Blackfoot Crossing, Red Crow pulled out the grass and gave it to the White officials and informed them that they will share the grass of the earth with them. Then he took some dirt from the earth and informed them that they could not share this part of the earth and what was underneath it, because it was put there by the Creator for the Indians' benefit and use.[23]

They understood that they would continue to have jurisdiction over the land and waters and the right to hunt and that certain portions of their land would be set aside and protected for their use as cattle ranches and farms in the event that the buffalo disappeared.

2.2.2 The Federal Crown's perspective on the purpose of Treaty 7

The Crown was driven to sign Treaties with the Blackfoot Confederacy by the desire to take control of the western frontier. The Crown intended that southern Alberta be put to similar uses as land south of the border that supported successful ranching operations. The presence of American traders compromised Canadian sovereignty and Canada was required to show the strength of its forces to keep American expansion in check. Part of MacDonald's plan in uniting Canada and facilitating its settlement was to construct a transcontinental railway, thus opening the area to immigrant settlement, but first a series of Treaties with the Indians of the territory needed to be finalized to ensure the safety of European immigrants.[24]

Besides securing peaceful settlement, treaty-making was viewed by the Crown as the final step in transferring of land for settlement to the Crown. Although the Crown had purchased Rupertsland from the Hudson's Bay Company by the *Rupertsland Transfer Agreement*, the *Royal Proclamation* of 1763 required that the Crown purchase the Indian interest in lands according to the prescribed process before subsequently granting those lands to settlers. Although the

---

[23] Louise Crop Eared Wolf, Blood, Treaty 7 Elders, *supra* note 7 at 114.

[24] As early as 1857, the British Government dispatched an expedition lead by Captain John Palliser to evaluate the economic potential of the lands between Red River and the Rocky Mountains. The Canadian government likewise, in the same year, sent out Henry Youle Hind with a similar mandate. Palliser and Hind determined that a fertile belt conducive to agriculture extended along the Red River and Assiniboine valleys and throughout the parkland region bordering the North Saskatchewan River. Palliser journeyed through the southern region in eastern Alberta during the middle of a drought cycle. He described the treeless prairies as being too arid for agricultural development. See Kinichi Matsui, *Reclaiming Indian Waters: Dams, Irrigation, and Indian Water Rights in Western Canada: 1858-1930*, PhD. Thesis (Vancouver: U.B.C., 2003) at 32-33.

language of the treaty is not the language of purchase, it does include the standard land cession clause found in all the numbered treaties, stating that the First Nation signatories:

> do hereby cede, release, surrender, and yield up to the Government of Canada for Her Majesty the Queen and her successors for ever, all their rights, titles, and privileges whatsoever to the lands included within the following limits...[25]

The territory ceded is then described as land bounded by certain rivers and bodies of water, suggesting that the Treaty territory may differ from Aboriginal territories. It is also unclear from the wording of the treaty that "rights, titles, and privileges" to water were ceded along with lands, a subject which will be dealt with below.

In addition to acquiring territory, the Crown further intended to secure Indian livelihood rights. In every territory entered by the Treaty Commissioners, the Indians voiced concerns for the loss of their traditional livelihood and for the means to make the transition to the new mode of living. The Crown consistently assured the Indians of its intention to protect hunting, fishing, and trapping throughout the territory ceded excepting those lands "taken up" as well as to assist with securing a modern livelihood through farming.

Treaty 7 was concluded the year following Treaty 6 "with a view to preserving the present friendly disposition of these tribes, which might easily give place to feelings of an unfriendly or hostile nature, should the treaty negotiations be much longer delayed."[26] The Crown's intention can also be ascertained by the conduct of the parties after Treaty signing. It is quite clear from the events immediately following the conclusion of Treaty 7 that one of the primary purposes of the Treaty was to assert British sovereignty in the west.

It appears that there is a common understanding between the Crown and Treaty 7 First Nations that the primary purpose of Treaty 7 was to establish law and order in the North-West Territories and to create peace between warring nations. With the Sioux uprising in the United States, Canada was afraid that war might likewise break out North of the 49th parallel. Although requested at various times to join the Sioux and the Cree in their campaign to wipe out the presence of Europeans, Crowfoot remained loyal to the Treaty of Peace signed in 1877 was able to restrain his young men from joining battle.

---

[25] Treaty No. 7, made 22nd Sept., 1877, between her Majesty the Queen and the Blackfeet and other Indian Tribes, at the Blackfoot Crossing of the Bow River, Fort Macleod (Ottawa: Queen's Printer and controller of Stationery, 1966).

[26] Morris, *supra* note 15.

In 1885, Treaty 7 First Nations were promised that the government would "always protect its faithful subjects, so long as they abided by the Treaty."[27] Crowfoot sent a telegram to Prime Minister MacDonald pledging his loyalty to the Crown. Clearly he viewed the Treaty as a solemn covenant for peaceful relations, not to be broken regardless of circumstances, as he was forced to choose between personal loyalty to his adopted son, Poundmaker, and political loyalty to the Crown:

> ...Should any Indians come to our reserve and ask us to join them in war, we will send them away. I have sent messengers to the Bloods and Piegans who belong to our treaty to tell them what we are doing and what we intend to do about the trouble...We will be loyal to the Queen whatever happens.[28]

Clearly, one of the priorities of Treaty 7 First Nations at the time of Treaty was to secure their interests along the rivers that supplied them with their livelihood. At the time of Treaty signing, Crowfoot suggested a common reserve for the Blackfoot, Bloods, and Sarcees. He asked Colonel Macleod to set aside land twenty miles upstream from Blackfoot Crossing, extending two hundred miles down the Bow River to its confluence with the Red Deer, and passing through the best hunting territories on the plains. A similar plot of land on the south side of the Bow River was set aside for ten years, to prevent traders from camping too close to the Indians and to stop them from building hunting shacks along the river where the buffalo grazed.[29]

It was some time before all the Treaty 7 First Nations settled on reserves. By the winter of 1878-1879 there were not enough buffalo in Canada to support Treaty 7 First Nations.[30] Edgar Dewdney responded to their request for assistance by bringing supplies to Blackfoot Crossing. There he found "about 1,300 Indians in a very destitute condition, and many on the verge of starvation."[31] A number of them went south of the border in search of remaining buffalo, only to return to finally settle and try their hands at agriculture and ranching.

---

[27] Calgary Herald, April 16, 1885 quoted in Dempsey, *supra* note 16 at 171.

[28] Crowfoot to Macdonald, April 11, 1885, in the Outgoing Telegrams from the North-West, 1885, at 107-108 quoted in Dempsey, *supra* note 16 at 172.

[29] *Ibid.* at 104-105; the reserves were ultimately surveyed in their present locations. The government denied including the rivers in any of the reserves.

[30] *Ibid.* at 111.

[31] Report of Edgar Dewdney to the superintendent general of Indian Affairs, Ottawa, January 2, 1880, in Sessional Papers of Canada, 1880, No. 46, at 78.

It is clear from the written records that the government and Treaty 7 First Nations had the common intention of creating peace on the prairies, although each had their own reasons. Both parties understood that a great change was about to take place and that a new relationship was required to move into a future of prosperity. It was also commonly understood that the finalization of a Treaty would open up the prairies of Southern Alberta to settlement. In exchange for allowing peaceful settlement, Treaty 7 First Nations were to receive assistance with pursuing both their traditional and modern livelihoods as they chose.

2.3   Application of the Principles of Treaty Interpretation to Treaty 7

When the principles of treaty interpretation are applied to Treaty 7 it is apparent that both the Crown and Treaty 7 First Nations intended to establish peaceful relations and protect First Nations livelihood, albeit they may have each had a different view in how these goals would be achieved. First Nations did not have any intention of ceding Aboriginal title to their territories, as they did not believe they had the power to grant land that had been given to their ancestors by the Creator. Given that the treaty terms must be interpreted in the sense that they would naturally have been understood by the Indians at the time of the signing,[32] land cession could not have been a common intention of the parties.

That being said, the Supreme Court stated clearly that the terms of the Treaty cannot be altered "[w]hile construing the language generously... by exceeding what "is possible on the language" or "realistic." However much First Nations may argue that Treaty 7 was not a land cession, the fact remains that the black letter of the treaty provided that the First Nations signatories have yielded up all their "rights titles and privileges" to the territories described. Furthermore, an interpretation of the numbered treaties as being anything other than land cessions would shake the legal foundations upon which Alberta has established its rights to resources. In theory, Treaties will be interpreted in a manner which maintains the integrity of the Crown. The honour of the Crown is presumed and no appearance of "sharp dealing" will be sanctioned. It could be argued that given the principle of the honour of the Crown, and the fact that there was no common understanding regarding land cession, Treaty 7 First Nations did not cede their Aboriginal title. However, practically speaking, while the cession clause of the treaty might be challenged, it is likely to be interpreted in such a way as to reconcile the divergent interpretations

---

[32]   *R. v. Badger, supra* note 5 at para 52.

without challenging the validity of the land cession.

One of the central disputes regarding treaty interpretation is over the allocation and use of natural resources, particularly water. The oral history of Treaty 7 reveals that the Aboriginal signatories perceived treaty-making as a means of protecting their livelihood through the sharing of their lands and resources. While the provincial government tends to argue that the treaty permits the taking up of lands for resource extraction, First Nations did not agree to allow the government to promote the depletion or degradation of water and aquatic ecosystems for the benefit of industrial or agricultural development. An examination of the terms of Treaty 7 sheds light on the environmental and natural resource rights of Treaty 7 signatories.

As discussed below, Treaty 7 did not extinguish Aboriginal rights, but rather protected Aboriginal practices, customs, and traditions exercised at the time of treaty-making. The Supreme Court has stated that these treaty-protected Aboriginal rights are dynamic and that the treaty protects traditional rights in their modern exercise. Identification of modern treaty rights involves determining what modern practice is an outgrowth of a Treaty right.

3. Did Treaty 7 Extinguish Aboriginal Rights and Title to Water?

To determine the effect of Treaty 7 on Aboriginal rights, it is necessary to apply two different tests: One to examine whether Treaty 7 extinguished Aboriginal title, and one to assess the effect of Treaty 7 on Aboriginal rights.

3.1 Extinguishment of Aboriginal Title

It has been argued that from First Nations' perspectives, their sovereignty and jurisdiction over their lands were recognized and affirmed in making treaties with the Crown. However, "[c]olonization theory interpreted the treaty purchases as extinguishing Aboriginal tenure and replacing it with Crown tenure."[33] Henderson, Benson, and Finlay have argued that

> The division of authority in the treaties between government and title reinforces the purpose of cession as a protective, not proprietary, nature. The chiefs and headmen did not transfer all the interests in the land.[34]

---

[33] J. Y. Henderson, M. L. Benson & I. M. Findlay, Aboriginal Tenure in the Constitution of Canada (Scarborough: Carswell, 2000) at 436.

[34] Ibid. at 443.

In coming to this conclusion the authors point out that British jurisprudence distinguishes the acquisition of territory, which is the subject matter of the right of sovereignty, from the acquisition of property, which is the subject matter of the right of ownership. The language of the treaties does not lend itself to interpretations supporting the Crown's acquisition of title and ownership, as there is no mention of "purchase." The Crown may have acquired territory under Treaty without acquiring property to the lands and waters, but even that is not clear from an Aboriginal perspective:

> ...in the treaties the Aboriginal tribes did not agree to the Crown's taking over their lands, nor did they agree to come under the control of the Crown. Under the vague term "settlement," there is no evidence in the treaty negotiation or text that the chiefs authorized the Crown to alienate their lands to others, or apply British land law within the ceded territory. On this basis, the Crown had no authority to use the land as a market commodity in the absence of discussing rents and profits from the land settlement.[35]

The source of Aboriginal title is the prior occupation of Canada by Aboriginal peoples. It is a legal right arising from occupation and possession of lands prior to the assertion of British sovereignty which pre-dated colonization and survived European claims to sovereignty.

Aboriginal title may only be extinguished by consent of First Nations. This rule is derived from the common law[36] and reinforced by the *Royal Proclamation of 1763,* which required that Indian lands be ceded collectively, willingly, and only to the Crown at a public meeting held for that purpose. The numbered treaties followed this formula, however, it is not clear from the reports of the treaty commissioners that it was always understood by First Nations that they were giving up their Aboriginal title to their lands.

Treaty 7 First Nations understood the primary purpose of Treaty 7 was to peacefully share the land with in-coming settlers. However, the British focus of the written Treaty 7 was the standard land cession clause:

> ...the Blackfeet, Blood, Piegan, Sarcee, Stony and other Indians inhabiting the district hereinafter more fully described and defined, do hereby cede, release, surrender, and yield up to the Government of Canada for Her Majesty the Queen and her successors for ever, all their rights, titles, and privileges whatsoever to the lands...

3.1.1 Test for Extinguishment of Aboriginal Title

---

[35] Ibid. at 441.

[36] *St. Catherine's Milling and Lumber Co.* v. *R.* (1877), 13 S.C.R. 577 at 612-13; *Calder* v. *A.G.B.C.* (1973), 34 D.L.R. (3d) 145 at 192 (S.C.C.).

It is usually taken for granted that this clause of the numbered treaties effectively extinguished Aboriginal title to land and waters appurtenant thereto based on the assumption that the very broadly-worded "cede, release and surrender" provision in the Treaties included rights to the beds of watercourses, despite the fact that water rights are not expressly mentioned, and despite the paucity of evidence that Aboriginal peoples intended to forever give up "all their rights title, privileges, whatsoever."[37]

There are several cases considering the 1923 treaties which decided that the "basket clause" or "cede, release, surrender" was effective. The signatories of the 1923 treaty were entirely competent and completely aware that the treaty was a land cession. The same could not be said about Treaty 7. The oral and written record shows that Crowfoot and Redcrow specifically requested that the land not be taken from them forever and either did not understand the effect of signing the treaty, or did not agree to land cession: They understood the treaty as an agreement for sharing the resources of the land. Moreover, Treaty 7 First Nations were not capable of making such a cession under their own legal systems.

According to the principles in *Delgamu'ukw*,[38] the treaty-making legal traditions of the Blackfoot confederacy must be given equal weight with the common law. Treaty 7 First Nations perceive Treaty 7 as setting the framework for sharing First Nations lands and resources and the Crown's wealth without compromising their legal interests. Their understanding that they would retain jurisdiction over their lands is reflected in last article of the treaty wherein the Blackfoot Confederacy agreed to "strictly observe this Treaty, and also to conduct and behave themselves as good and loyal subjects of Her Majesty the Queen." Furthermore, they promised to

> obey and abide by the Law, that they will maintain peace and good order between each other and between themselves and other tribes of Indians, and between themselves and others of Her Majesty's subjects…and that they will assist the officers of Her Majesty in bringing to justice and punishment any Indian offending against the stipulations of this Treaty, or infringing the laws in force in the country so ceded.

Even if Treaty 7 First Nations accepted the assertion of Crown sovereignty, which is not supported by either the written or oral record, the Chiefs retained jurisdiction, including the power to make and enforce the law, throughout their territories. The Crown's view of complete

---

[37] *Mikisew Cree First Nation* v. *Canada (Minister of Canadian Heritage)*, [2005] S.C.J. No. 71 (QL); 2005 SCC 69 at para 2; *Badger, supra* note 5; *R.* v. *Sundown*, [1999] 1 S.C.R. 393; [1999] S.C.J. No.13 (QL).

[38] *Delgamu'ukw* v. *British Columbia*, [1997] S.C.J. No. 108 (QL); [1997] 3 S.C.R. 1010.

surrender of all legal rights is inherently incompatible with Treaty 7 First Nations' view of the treaty.

It is evident from Alberta water policies and regulations that the provincial Crown takes the position that the cession clause was effective in extinguishing all Aboriginal title, and specifically title to the waterbeds, in the "tracts surrendered." However, in applying the principles of treaty interpretation which require common intent and understanding, we can conclude that there was no shared intent with regard to the surrender of lands and resources.

3.1.2 Did the Cession of Land Include Title to the Riverbeds?

Assuming that Treaty 7 did result in a land cession to the crown, at the time of Treaty, two presumptions may have operated, unbeknownst to Treaty 7 First Nations, affecting their interests in the rivers and waters upon which they relied. At common law it was presumed that a general transfer included all waters appurtenant to the land unless expressly excluded, and transfers of land along rivers included the bed of the rivers *ad medium filum aquae*. The provincial and federal governments take the position that Treaty 7 extinguished Aboriginal title to water and the waterbeds and that the riverbeds do not form part of the reserves.

Whether the date of assertion of sovereignty was 1763, 1869 or 1877, the common law at the time of assertion of British sovereignty was that riparian owners owned the beds of streams *ad medium filum aquae*. Assuming that the common law applied without exception at the time of Treaty 7, title to waterbeds was either not ceded by Treaty, or if it was, reserves included waterbeds *ad medium filum aquae*.[39]

3.1.3 Title to Water, Waterbeds and Watercourses Runs Separately from the land

Even if Treaty 7 did effect the cession of land, Supreme Court decisions regarding land transfers suggest that title to the waters and waterbeds may not have been included with the ceded land. If Aboriginal title to water runs separately from the land, Aboriginal title to water and waterbeds may continue to exist independent of Aboriginal title to land generally and title to Treaty 7 reserves.

However, there is a common law presumption that a general conveyance of land passes all interests except those specifically reserved in the deed or transfer. In *Blueberry River Indian*

---

[39] The question of whether treaty reserves include the riverbeds is dealt with more fully below.

Band v. *Canada*[40] the Supreme Court rejected the Crown's main argument that "the mineral rights were transferred, not because anyone intended them to be transferred, but by reason of the presumption of law that a general conveyance of land passes all interests *except those specifically reserved in the deed or transfer* (emphasis mine)."[41] McLachlin J. noted mineral rights can be severed from surface rights or realty and form the basis of a separate chain of title. Because water is analogous to oil, the ruling in *Blueberry* would suggest that Aboriginal title to water may not have passed in the general land cession, without intention to do so.

Parliament passed the *Northwest Irrigation Act*[42] in 1894, fully seventeen years after Treaty 7 was signed, severing riparian lands from rights to water, preferring instead to allocate water through a water licencing system based on prior appropriation. The British common law presumption at the time of Treaty was that the waterbed passed with the land to the centre of the stream.[43] Although there is no agreement as to whether the common law applied to the then Northwest Territories, particularly in relation to navigable streams, the courts of Alberta have applied this presumption to non-navigable streams in the province.[44] Assuming that Treaty 7 was a land cession treaty and that this common law principle can be applied to land cessions by First Nations, the reference in the "cede, release and surrender" provision to "all rights, titles and privileges whatsoever to the lands" would be deemed to include not only cession of the land itself, but the waters appurtenant to lands surrendered. Likewise, reserve lands set aside would have included riverbeds *ad medium filum aquae*.

This presumption has since been denied in *Nikal*[45], where the Court held that the common law presumption did not apply and the presumption *ad medium filum aquae* did not apply to navigable streams. While this case is distinguishable, it raises the issue of when the common law presumption applied to transfers of land at the time of treaty. It would appear from the text of Treaty 7 that the Crown recognized First Nations rights to the riverbed and waters when it expressly reserved the right of navigation as a separate right. If the presumption ceased to apply after Treaty 7, the Crown may have obtained title to the riverbeds *ad medium filum aquae* and

---

[40] [1995] 4 S.C.R. 344, 130 D.L.R. (4th) 193, [1996] 2 C.N.L.R. 25, 190 N.R. 89, 102 F.T.R. 160.

[41] *Ibid*.

[42] S.C. 1894, c.30.

[43] *Johnston* v. *O'Neill*, [1911] A.C. 552 (H.L.).

[44] *Flewelling* v. *Johnston* (1921), 59 D.L.R. 419 (Alta. S.C., A.D.), [1921] 2 W.W.R. 374.

[45] *R.* v. *Nikal*, [1996] 1 S.C.R. 1013; [1996] S.C.J. No. 47 (QL).

reserves boundaries would have extended *ad medium filum aquae*. If the presumption ceased to apply before Treaty 7, the Crown would have already assumed title of navigable streams. This seems to directly conflict with the Blackfoot Confederacy's understanding of the Treaty.

Delgamuukw, Guerin, and more recently, *Osoyoos*[46], confirm that Aboriginal title to traditional lands and title to reserve lands are to be treated the same way. *Delgamuukw* further establishes that the statutory regime governing reserve lands is relevant to defining the nature and content of Aboriginal title generally,[47] and that Aboriginal title includes mineral title, although mineral title runs separately from title to land. By analogy, Aboriginal title also includes title to waterbeds and waters, despite the fact that such title is severable from title to the land.

In *Blueberry*, the Supreme Court held that First Nations' intentions regarding the surrender of mineral rights must be clear and based on full, free and informed consent. McLachlin J. emphasized that the evidence in that case established that mineral rights had never been mentioned or considered by the Band in relation to the transaction in question. The failure of the conveyance document to exclude mineral rights constituted a weak and ultimately insufficient evidentiary basis for finding that the Band had the necessary intention to surrender its mineral title. The Court stated that when "the written source is silent where one would have expected clear wording" to transfer title, and "the oral testimony establishes that the issue was never even discussed", this silence, "cannot be evidence of intention" to cede their title.[48]

The Treaty was silent regarding the transfer of water and it appears from the oral testimony that the transfer of the waters and waterbeds was never discussed. McLachlin J.'s observations in *Blueberry* that "the Indians were unsophisticated and may not have fully understood the concept of different interests in land and how they might be lost," and that "they were never advised of the transfer of [their] mineral rights" are also directly pertinent to the issue of title to water at the time of Treaty. The Court's insistence in *Blueberry* on an express and independent surrender of mineral title rejects any presumption that a generally-framed surrender of all interests in traditional lands necessarily includes water which, like minerals, attach to the land.

---

[46] *Osoyoos Indian Band* v. *Oliver (Town),* [2001] S.C.J. No. 82; 2001 SCC 85; [2001] 3 S.C.R. 746.

[47] As seen in the passage from *Delgamuukw* quoted earlier, Lamer C.J. expressly referred to the *Blueberry* decision and the Court's reliance on the *Indian Act* in that case to bolster his own use of the *Indian Oil and Gas Act* as a basis for concluding that the Aboriginal interest in reserve lands includes mineral rights.

[48] Emphasis added.

In the *Osoyoos* case, land had been removed from the reserve under s.35 of the *Indian Act* to build a canal for the neighboring town. That section allowed the expropriation of Indian lands in the public interest. One of the questions before the Court was what interest in land had actually been transferred, as the Order in Council effecting the transfer had been vague and ambiguous. The majority of the Supreme Court clearly affirmed *Delgamu'ukw*'s earlier holding that Aboriginal title and the Aboriginal interest in reserve land are equal and "in a category of their own," being "*sui generis* interests in land that are distinct from 'normal' proprietary interests."[49] Furthermore, "traditional principles of the common law relating to property may not be helpful in the context of aboriginal interests in land." Because reserve land does not fit neatly within the rationale underlying the law of compulsory takings, and because the Aboriginal interest in land has important cultural components, courts must " 'go beyond the usual restrictions imposed by the common law,' in order to give effect to the true purpose of dealings relating to reserve land".[50] Moreover, because the Crown owes a fiduciary duty to the band, a clear and plain intention to remove lands from the reserve must be evident. The Court concluded, applying the principle of minimal impairment, that although there had been a transfer in the interest in land, it amounted to the granting of a statutory easement, leaving the canal lands "in the reserve."

A number of key propositions emerge from the Supreme Court's decisions in *Delgamuukw*, *Blueberry* and *Osoyoos* that suggest that Aboriginal title to water was not extinguished by Treaty 7. Among other things these cases demonstrate that extinguishment of title to water and waterbeds must be clear, express, and based on full, free, and informed consent. Furthermore, these case demonstrate that clear words specific to extinguishment of title to water is required: General language and the fact that the matter was never discussed cannot be taken as evidence of the intention to extinguish title to water. Finally, it is clear from these cases that First Nations' intention must be considered. At the time of Treaty, Treaty Seven First Nations would have relied on their own legal tradition of Treaty-making and would not have appreciated the British common law relating to land transfers.

---

[49]   *Osoyoos supra* note 45.

[50]   *Ibid.* at para 43, referring to *St. Mary's Indian Band* v. *Cranbrook (City)*, [1997] 2 S.C.R. 657, aff'g [1996] 2 C.N.L.R. 222 and *Blueberry, supra* note 39 at para. 7, per Gonthier J.

Woven together, these various threads from recent Supreme Court of Canada jurisprudence provide a strong basis for challenging the effectiveness of the "cede, release and surrender" provisions in extinguishing Aboriginal title to water.

3.2 Extinguishment of Aboriginal Rights

The Court in *Sparrow*, adopted the test for extinguishment stated by Hall J. in *Calder*[51]: The Crown has the onus to prove that it was Sovereign's clear and plain intention to extinguish an Aboriginal right prior to 1982.[52] Aboriginal rights may have been extinguished by treaty provided this test has been met. As discussed below, Treaty 7 does not meet the test of clear and plain intent to extinguish Aboriginal water rights and title to water in their entirety. The question is, then what Aboriginal and treaty rights to water continue to exist after Treaty 7 and did subsequent legislation or Crown policy extinguish them in part or in whole?

There is no clear and plain intention in Treaty 7 to limit or extinguish Blackfoot uses of water. In *Adams*, the Crown relied on the surrender of lands around the fishing area as demonstrating "clear and plain" intention to extinguish the Aboriginal right to fish. The Court found this evidence to be insufficient proof.[53] In coming to this decision, the Court explained that the surrender of proprietary interests in the land is separate from "the free-standing aboriginal right to fish for food which existed in the waters adjacent to those lands."[54]

> There is no evidence to suggest what the parties to the surrender agreement, including the Crown, intended with regards to the right of the Mohawks to fish in the area; absent such evidence the *Sparrow* test for extinguishment cannot be said to have been met."[55]

Thus Aboriginal rights, that have their roots in pre-contact distinctive Aboriginal practices, customs, and traditions, may exist independent of land cession Treaties. Aboriginal rights to water, in so far as they are related to Aboriginal practices, customs, and traditions, may continue to exist as free-standing rights in the wake of extinguishment of title to the beds of lakes and watercourses. Aboriginal rights and title may have survived Treaty 7 and may have been

---

[51] *Calder, supra* note 35.
[52] *R. v. Sparrow*, [1990] 1 S.C.R. 1075; [1990] S.C.J. No. 49 at para 37.
[53] *R. v. Adams*, [1996] 3 S.C.R. 101; 138 D.L.R. (4th) 657; 202 N.R. 89; 110 C.C.C. (3d) 97; [1996] 4 C.N.L.R. 1.
[54] *Ibid.*
[55] *Ibid.*

afforded more protection under treaty. Furthermore, Treaty 7 may have created new rights for Aboriginal signatories or altered existing rights. The only way to ascertain what rights existed after entering into Treaty is to inquire into the meaning of Treaty 7.

4. Rights to Water Under Treaty 7

As set out in the previous chapter, the Blackfoot Confederacy possessed Aboriginal rights to draw water from rivers and streams for drinking, washing, tanning hides, watering horses, and other domestic purposes prior to entering into Treaty. They also possessed the right to use the waters for transportation and for ceremonial purposes. All of these uses of water supported their Aboriginal lifestyle as buffalo hunters on the plains. Furthermore, it was determined in the previous chapter that the Blackfoot Confederacy had Aboriginal title to the waters within their Aboriginal territories.

Water rights and their cession or retention, with the exception of the Queen's right of navigation, were not clearly enumerated in the written terms of Treaty 7. Water, essential to all life, was a necessity to ensuring both parties' prosperity. The Crown must have intended to use water for future developments, such as irrigation and transportation, and First Nations must have assumed that they would continue to have unfettered access to the rivers, streams, and groundwater that nourished them and their stock since time immemorial. Failure to directly address the issue of the transfer of water raises a question about the lack of shared intent and the meaning of Treaty rights to water. Complete silence on the issue of water implies that no agreement with regard to water was reached, unless it can be inferred that references to lands included the waters appurtenant to them.

To ascertain the nature of Treaty 7 promises relating to water rights, it is necessary to apply the principles of Treaty interpretation. Assuming that waters were included in references to land, extinguishment of Aboriginal title to the waters may be reasonably incidental to the extinguishment of Aboriginal title to the land under the territorial clause. However, a right to use of or access to water may be reasonably incidental to the livelihood rights guaranteed under Treaty.[56]

The Crown is obligated by its honour to fulfill its promises:

---

[56] *Sundown, supra* note 36; *Simon v. The Queen*, [1985] 2 S.C.R. 387.

the honour of the Crown was pledged to the fulfilment of its obligations to the Indians. This had been the Crown's policy as far back as the *Royal Proclamation of 1763*, and is manifest in the promises recorded in the report of the Commissioners.[57]

Among the promises made relating to water resources were: livelihood rights, hunting rights, and the right to a reserve.

4.1 The Treaty Right to a Livelihood

It is clear that the protection of livelihood rights formed part of the common intention of the parties during Treaty negotiations. The written terms of Treaty 7 included specific, but regulated, protection of the "avocation of hunting" and the promise of assistance with agricultural pursuits. Reserves were created to protect the traditional livelihood of Treaty 7 First Nations.

Brian Slattery argues that

> Where a treaty recognizes and guarantees aboriginal rights, it does not convert them into treaty rights, in the absence of very clear language to that effect. <u>Treaty rights throw a protective mantle over aboriginal rights, providing an extra layer of security</u>. The latter become "treaty-protected" aboriginal rights...(emphasis added)[58]

Far from extinguishing rights to exercise Aboriginal practices, customs, and traditions, Treaty 7 cast a "protective mantle" over Aboriginal rights, including the right to use water.

4.1.1 The Treaty Right to a Traditional Livelihood

The traditional livelihood rights of Treaty 7 First Nations were protected under Treaty 7. Commissioner Laird reported "They were also assured that their liberty of hunting over the open prairie would not be interfered with, so long as they did not molest settlers and others in the country."[59] To protect Treaty 7 first Nations' livelihood rights, Laird promised that "the Great Mother" would pass a law "to prevent them from being destroyed."[60] The written Treaty promised First Nations "the right to pursue their vocations of hunting throughout the Tract

---

[57] *Mikisew, supra* note 36 at para 51.

[58] *Simon, supra* note 55 at 812-16; *Marshall, supra* note 4 at para 47; Brian Slattery, "Making Sense of Aboriginal and Treaty Rights" [2000] 79 Can. Bar Rev. 196 at 210.

[59] Report by David Laird, Lieutenant-Governor and Special Indian Commissioner, in Morris, *supra* note 15 at 257.

[60] Report from the Globe correspondent (17October 1877) in Morris, *supra* note 15 at 267-8. Morris commented: "…a report of the speeches of the Commissioners and Indians, extracted from a report in the Globe newspaper, dated October 4th, 1877, which, though not authentic, I believe, gives a general view of what passed during the negotiations" Morris, *supra* note 15 at 250.

surrendered" albeit "subject to such regulations as may, from time to time, be made by the Government of the country." Hunting rights would not extend to "such Tracts as may be required or taken up from time to time for settlement, mining, trading or other purposes" by the Government.

The Commissioners, in promising to protect Treaty 7 First Nations' traditional livelihood by buffalo hunting, appear to have anticipated the end of intensive buffalo hunting as the primary means of livelihood. Annuities, relief rations, and ammunition were meant to sustain Treaty 7 First Nations in their traditional livelihood for the short term while they made the transition to agrarian farming.[61]

It follows that rights such as the right to hunt and the right to a livelihood were afforded added protection by the Treaty. It matters little that part of the government's "game plan" in affording Treaty protection to Aboriginal rights was to persuade First Nations to embrace civilization and to force them to settle on reserves in an effort to transform them into yeoman farmers.[62] If the Aboriginal right to hunt is a "treaty-protected" Aboriginal right, Treaty 7 First Nations have incidental rights to access and use water, regardless of whether the waterbeds were 'ceded', to enable them to exercise their right to hunt. Such uses would include transportation, drinking, and other domestic uses. It may be further argued that the aquatic environment must be of such a quality as to sustain wildlife that would ensure the continuing viability of Treaty 7 First Nations hunting lifestyle. If the water is so contaminated as to destroy the livelihood of First Nations, this may constitute a breach of the Blackfoot Confederacy's treaty-protected aboriginal right to hunt.

4.1.2 The Treaty Right to a Modern Livelihood

The British written accounts of the Treaty clearly indicate the intention of First Nations and the Crown to establish cattle ranching and agricultural operations along the rivers chosen by Treaty 7 First Nations and to facilitate the continuation of traditional hunting, and trapping practices along river valleys.

---

[61] Frank J. Tough, "The Forgotten Constitution: The Natural Resources Transfer Agreements and Indian Livelihood Rights, CA. 1925-1933" 2004 41 Alta. L. Rev. 999.

[62] Livelihood rights are more fully dealt with in Chapter 6.

Despite the promise to protect Indian traditional livelihood, the Commissioners were aware that the days of buffalo hunting were numbered. They expanded their promise to include a commitment to help the Indians in making the transition to a new mode of livelihood, specifically ranching:

> But in a very few years the buffalo will probably be all destroyed, and for this reason the Queen wishes to help you to live in the future in some other way. She wishes you to allow her white children to come and live on your land and raise cattle, and should you agree to this she will assist you to raise cattle and grain, and thus give you the means of living when the buffalo are no more.

The written terms of the Treaty indicate that the intention was to establish ranches and farms on reserve.[63]

Minister of the Interior, Hon. David Mills in his Annual Report for 1877 speculated that the First Nations within Treaty 7 territory "are unlikely to become farmers, but as the country they inhabit presents unusual facilities for that industry, they may be induced to adopt a pastoral life. They already possess large herds of horses, and may be taught to raise cattle also."[64]

Laird reported that cattle ranching would likely succeed in the Treaty 7 territory:

> The land around the fort, and indeed for almost the whole distance between the Bow and Old Man's Rivers, is well adapted for grazing; and where cultivation has been fairly attempted this season, grain and vegetables have been a success.[65]

Shortly after signing the treaty, the government breached the treaty promise to assist Treaty 7 First Nations in making the transition to self-sustaining farmers and ranchers. When they were experiencing their greatest desperate need Dewdney advised them to go into the United States in search of buffalo:

> I advised them strongly to go and gave them some provisions to take them off. They continued to follow the Buffalo further and further south until they reached the main herd and there they remained...I consider their remaining away saved the Govt. $100,000 at least.[66]

A few weeks after their return to Canada, Crowfoot resigned himself and his people to the agricultural way of life.

---

[63] Morris, *supra* note 15 at 250.

[64] Morris, *supra* note 15 at 246-7.

[65] Morris, *supra* note 15 at 255.

[66] Edgar Dewdney to D.L. McPherson, August 4, 1881, in the Macdonald Papers, Vol. 210, 242-3.

The Treaty Commissioners had undertaken to "encourage the practice of agriculture among the Indians" and to assist in the development of a ranching and farming economy. The terms of Treaty 7 and the facts surrounding the establishment of Treaty 7 reserves strongly suggest that the Crown intended to provide lands suitable for agricultural purposes to assist Treaty 7 First Nations in making the transition from a subsistence livelihood to agriculture. Without access to the waters of the rivers, most of the land within the reserves would not be suitable for agriculture. Therefore, it is reasonable to conclude that Treaty 7, by implication, secures water rights for agricultural and ranching purposes as well as a sufficient quantity of water to irrigate reserve lands.

4.2 The Treaty Right to a Reserve

The right to a reserve was a new right created by Treaty 7, the purpose of which is closely connected to the livelihood rights protected under treaty. Reserves were created in part to encourage First Nations to make the transition from buffalo hunters to settled farmers and ranchers. While the right to hunt requires a supply of clean water and a healthy aquatic and riparian environment to facilitate resource use, the right to a reserve implies a proprietary interest in the bed of watercourses. This proprietary interest is *sui generis* in nature, but may be similar to that of common law riparian owners. If that is the case, First Nations may have a more solid and direct right to the undisturbed quality, quantity, and flow of water on reserve. The question remains whether reserve lands include ownership of the bed of the river *ad medium filum aquae*.

4.2.1 The Treaty Right to Water Appurtenant to a Reserve

Treaty 7 First Nations maintain that their reserves include the rivers running appurtenant to them. The Crown, however, surveyed Treaty 7 reserves so as to exclude the rivers. By applying the principles of Treaty interpretation it is possible to determine the purpose of establishing the reserves in Treaty 7 territory and to ascertain whether reserves included *sui generis* or riparian ownership of the waterbeds appurtenant to the reserve. "[T]he wording of the Treaty, the record of negotiations and the surrounding historical context" are essential to determining the common intention of the parties in setting aside reserves at the time the treaties were negotiated and executed.[67]

At the time of Treaty, Commissioner Laird had promised that "a reserve of land will be set apart for yourselves and your cattle, upon which none others will be permitted to encroach..."[68] The Commissioner's Report indicates that the Indians were aware of their continuing need for an adequate water supply for various purposes. In allotting the reserves, Lieut.-Col. McLeod spoke to the Chiefs at their camps and they chose the localities of their reserves.[69] Significantly, each Treaty 7 First Nation chose a locality along a river. Their choice of land and the rivers running appurtenant to them were inferentially entered into the Treaty document by their choice of reserve lands.

Clearly, water rights were crucial to the establishment of agriculture and ranching. A.S. Williams, in his capacity as a legal officer,[70] wrote to Duncan Campbell Scott recommending recognition of on-reserve water rights:

> the rights of Indians in Canada to have water for domestic, agricultural and irrigation purposes must practically stand upon the same footing as that of the Indians of the Unites States...The avowed purpose of the Crown when making treaties with Indians, as shown by the policy of this treatment of them extending over many years, was and is to encourage Indians in habit of industry and to induce them to engage in pastural [sic] pursuits and in the cultivation of the soil in order that they may not only become self-supporting but that they may eventually take up the habits and busy themselves with the enterprise of civilized people...[71]

Early in the development of water law in the west, H. W. Grunsky, legal advisor for the Dominion Water Power Branch concluded that it was:

> fair to assume that when the Indian reserves were created, waters required by the Indians for domestic, irrigation, and other purposes went with the lands, <u>irrespective of any provincial statutes relating to the recording of water rights</u>.(emphasis mine)[72]

---

[67] *Lac La Ronge Indian Band* v. *Canada,* 2002 CarswellSask 626; [2002] 4 C.N.L.R. iv (note); 302 N.R. 197 (note); 241 Sask. R. 78 (note); 313 W.A.C. 78 (note) at para 154.

[68] It was not until 1881, upon returning starving and disappointed from chasing diminishing buffalo herds, that Crowfoot and the Blackfoot were finally ready to choose and settle on their reserve: Indian Agent N.T. Macleod to Lieutenant Governor Dewdney, Fort Macleod, June 1, 1881, in the Blood Correspondence, Vol. 1, 89.

[69] Morris, *supra* note 15 at 259.

[70] A.S. Williams later became Deputy Superintendent of Indian Affairs.

[71] A.S. Williams to Duncan Campbell Scott, 27 July 1920, RG10, vol. 3660, File 9755-4.

[72] Grunsky to Challies, 5 September 1919, RG10, vol. 3660, File 9755-4.

Treaty 7 is silent on the issue of whether the area of land set aside for Treaty 7 First Nations reserves included the beds of the rivers. The written treaty expressly delegated or reserved to the Crown "the right to navigate the above mentioned rivers, to land and receive fuel cargos on the shores and banks thereof, to build bridges and establish ferries thereon, to use the fords thereof…" The necessary implication to be drawn from this language is that the Crown intended to use the rivers for navigation purposes, but it is not clear that the bed of the rivers were granted as part of the Blackfoot, Blood, and Sarcee reserves. Similar clauses were not included for the rivers of appurtenant to the Peigan or Stoney reserves. The absence of clear language in the treaty implies that the English drafters did not intend to exclude the beds of the rivers from the reserve. The only clear intention is that the Crown use the river for navigation, construction of bridges, or other such purposes. The *contra proferentum* rule of construction set out by the Supreme Court in *Nowegijick* supports the idea that, if the Crown had intended to exclude the bed of the Bow River from the reserve, it would have stated this intention in clear and express terms in the treaty. Moreover, it is an established principle of Treaty interpretation that any ambiguity in the survey documents must be resolved in favour of Treaty 7 First Nations.

4.2.1.1 The Effect of the Common Law Rule of *ad medium filum aquae*

It may be anticipated that *Nikal* and *Lewis*[73] will be used to refute the argument that reserves include title to the riverbeds of navigable streams. These cases applied the *ad medium filum aquae* presumption to the creation of reserves. It is a common law rule by which ownership of the bed of non-tidal river or stream belongs in equal halves to the owners of riparian lands. The English common law rule is as follows:

> ... the owner of land through which a non-tidal stream flows owns the bed of the stream unless it has been expressly or impliedly reserved; and if the stream forms the boundary between lands owned by different persons, each proprietor owns the bed of the river ad medium filum aquae -- to the centre thread of the stream.[74]

In *Lewis,* the Court considered whether the Squamish River was included within the boundaries of the reserve and concluded that it was not, having considered that it was the Crown's policy to treat Indians and non-Indians equally as to the use of the water and not to grant

---

[73] *R. v. Lewis,* [1996] 1 S.C.R. 921; [1996] S.C.J. No. 46 (QL).

[74] G. V. La Forest, Water Law in Canada: The Atlantic Provinces, Dept. of Regional Economic Expansion (1973) at pp. 241-42 (Hereinafter LaForest).

exclusive use of any public waters for the purpose of fishing. The *ad medium filum aquae* presumption did not apply to the creation of the reserve because it does not apply in western Canada to navigable rivers.

In *R.* v. *Nikal*,[75] the Supreme Court considered whether an Indian reserve spanning both sides of a river, non-navigable at the site of the reserve, included the bed of the river *ad medium filum aquae*. The Court concluded that the presumption *ad medium filum aquae* could not apply to navigable rivers in Canada because Crown title superseded private rights where waterways were used for public navigation. The Court reasoned that courts in western Canada had not applied the presumption *ad medium filum aquae* to navigable rivers as a matter of policy. The Court accepted the argument that title to the waterbeds of navigable waters vested in the Crown from at least 1869, even without first extinguishing Aboriginal title.[76] The Court justified exemption of navigable waters from the common law rule stating that:

> In a country occupied from the earliest days by hunters, trappers, fishers and traders whose main and almost exclusive highways were the rivers and streams, such laws were contrary to the requirements and necessities of the whole community.[77]

Without any consideration of the Royal Proclamation of 1763 which requires cession of Aboriginal title to the Crown by Treaty, the Court declared that, "In this country the public right of navigation and of fishery in all navigable waters *has always existed and been recognised.* The Court reasoned that public rights in all navigable rivers "have been deemed always existent in the Crown *ex jure naturae,* so that the title in the bed thereof remained in the Crown after it had made grants of land bordering upon the banks of such rivers, the doctrine of *ad medium filum aquae* not applying thereto." [78] So long as the waters "are navigable in fact, whether or not the waters are tidal or non-tidal, the public right of navigation exists" as is the case for the Oldman River.[79]

---

[75] *R.* v. *Nikal,* [1996] 1 S.C.R. 1013; [1996] S.C.J. No. 47 (QL).

[76] *Re Iverson and Greater Winnipeg Water District,* (1921), 57 D.L.R. 184 at 202-3.

[77] *Ibid.*

[78] *Ibid.*

[79] *Friends of the Oldman River Society* v. *Canada (Minister of Transport)* [1992] 1 S.C.R. 3, at p. 54 per La Forest J.

To assess navigability, the entire length of the river from its mouth to the point where its navigability terminates must be considered.[80] A whole river or lake may be regarded as navigable "even though at some point navigation may be impossible or possible only for small craft by reason of rapids or shoals."[81] The court concluded in applying this criteria, where a river is navigable, the *ad medium filum aquae* presumption has no application. "On this basis alone" the Court felt that "it can be concluded that reserve does not include the river."[82]

Nikal presents some problems for Treaty 7 First Nations, however it may be distinguished. First, *Nikal* was decided in the context of an Aboriginal right to fish in an area not covered by treaty: The lands and rivers described fell outside the boundaries of Rupertsland, the territory covered by the *Royal Proclamation of 1763*, and a reserve had been granted without first extinguishing Aboriginal title to the land. Therefore, the Court did not explore First Nations understanding by applying the principles of treaty interpretation and considering the historical context or the common intention of the parties regarding the protection of Aboriginal rights to livelihood and water use.

Second, although an argument was made that the reserve included title to the riverbed *ad medium filum aquae*, the Court did not apply full analysis of the existence of Aboriginal title, nor did the Court consider how exemption from the common law presumption served to reconcile pre-sovereignty occupation by Aboriginal people with the sovereignty of the Crown. The framework for analysis of Aboriginal title claims was not released by the Supreme Court of Canada until two years later in the *Delgamu'ukw* decision. It can only be hoped that, had *Nikal* been decided after *Delgamu'ukw*, it would have at least recognized the possibility of unextinguished Aboriginal title to the riverbed.

Nikal and *Lewis* may summarize the Crown's intent to assert sovereignty over navigable streams, but these cases did not consider the continuing jurisdiction of First Nations over their territories. Treaty 7 First Nations specifically allowed the right of navigation to the Queen without surrendering jurisdiction. Furthermore, the *North-West Territories Act* may have exempted Canada from applying the common law rule of *ad medium filum aquae* in Canada, but

---

[80] *Nikal, supra* note 74 at para 73.

[81] LaForest, *supra* 73 note at 181.

[82] *Nikal, supra* note 74 at para 74.

that *Act* was passed a full eleven years after Treaty 7 was signed and after most if, not all, of the reserve lands were surveyed.

These considerations, coupled with the *contra preferendum* rule, raise the question of whether the Crown would have been legally capable of excluding the rivers from the reserves when they were surveyed. If Treaty 7 First Nations understood that their livelihood would be protected by the creation of reserves, and if their livelihood depended in large part on the availability of water for hunting, farming, and ranching, and if they specifically chose their reserves along certain rivers (as was the case for Crowfoot who initially chose a reserve along the Bow), then the riverbeds and waters cannot be excluded from the reserves.

4.2.2 The Crown's Assumption of Title to Navigable Streams

As discussed above, the Crown may have acquired rights in territory without acquiring rights in property. The language of Treaty 7 indicates that the treaty officially granted the Queen and her subjects the right of navigation without granting title to the rivers and waterbeds. Treaty 7 clearly distinguishes the right of navigation from title to the rivers:

> ...reserving to Her Majesty, as may now or hereafter be required by Her for the use of Her Indian and other subjects, from all the Reserves hereinbefore described, the right to navigate the above mentioned rivers, to land and receive fuel cargoes on the shores and banks thereof, to build bridges and establish ferries thereon, to use the fords thereof and all the trails leading thereto...[83]

The black letter of the Treaty appears to reinforce the continuing existence of Aboriginal title to waterbeds and waterways.

It could be argued that exclusive ownership of navigable waterways would be difficult to prove given Canada's long history of traders and travelers employing the natural waterways as highways of commerce.[84] Research would be required to inquire further into the extent that the waters of Southern Alberta were used as public highways. It would appear from the historical record that the preferred mode of transportation of the Blackfoot was by horseback, as horses allowed them to follow the movements of the buffalo.[85] The Hudson's Bay Company did not have a strong presence in Southern Alberta, the traders doing business with First Nations, at least

---

[83] Treaty 7, *supra* note 24.

[84] It has been argued that Canada has had exclusive ownership of navigable streams since 1869 – *Nikal*.

[85] See generally, Dempsey, *supra* note 16.

before the presence of the N.W.M.P., were transient American traders. Even after forts were established on the prairies, supplies were brought in overland to the Forts by Metis freighters traveling with Red River carts.

The assertion of British sovereignty in Canada, assuming it was 1869, the year Rupertsland was transferred to Canada, pre-dates the use of navigable waters as public highways. Even if the date of the assertion of sovereignty is as late as 1877, the date of Treaty, navigable streams were not used as public highways, except for use in the fur trade and then largely by Cree middlemen. David Mandelbaum has suggested that the river systems were historically used as highways for trade. [86] Safe passage through enemy territories was allowed by the operation of Blackfoot treaty laws.

Special permission was granted for the safe passage of the Queen and her subjects. It could be argued that Treaty 7 First Nations, by signing Treaty 7, intended to assert their title to their territories while allowing safe passage by the Queen in exchange for protection and assistance. In the case of non-navigable waterways, Aboriginal title might be easier to establish.[87]

If equal weight is given to the common law and Aboriginal legal perspectives, it is seriously open to question whether either the common law presumption *ad medium filum aquae* or that the incorporation of the common law "except as where appropriate" with the effect of exempting navigable streams from the *ad medium filum aquae* presumption could have ever applied to Aboriginal title lands. A determination of the existence of Aboriginal title is never so simple as a mere recitation of existing common law principles. There must always be a consideration of Aboriginal legal perspectives, which is impossible without an inquiry into the language, land tenure, culture, and social organization of the Aboriginal group in question.

It is legally possible for water rights to run separately from the land. The specific protection of the Queen's right to navigate on some reserves appears to add credence to the view

---

[86] See generally David G. Mandelbaum, *The Plains Cree* (New York : AMS Press, 1979): by 1763, the Cree, acting as middlemen in the fur trade traveled along watercourses as far east as Montreal and as far west as the Saskatchewan River. European presence followed the Cree. Other prairie peoples were less interested in the fur trade as long as buffalo were plentiful on the prairies. The Cree "were a canoe-using people and so were readily able to utilize the network of waterways in their terrain to transport the raw materials to the posts. This trait influenced their later status as middlemen. Their...ability to travel by canoe, gave them a great advantage over the more distant people who lacked... the technique of water transport."

[87] Kenneth J. Tyler, "The Division of Powers and Aboriginal Water Rights Issues": National Symposium on Water Law, Environmental Law CLE Programme, 1999, unpublished.

that Treaty 7 First Nations did not generally give up water rights under the Treaty: They merely agreed to share jurisdiction. Therefore, it follows that, although the Treaty may have been a general transfer or cession, it was the intention of Treaty 7 First Nations to retain water rights throughout their transferred lands and in particular to those waters appurtenant to the reserves.

Even if the Court was correct in *Nikal*, that title to the beds of navigable waters rests with the Crown, free-standing Aboriginal rights to water use having their origin in pre-contact practices, customs, and traditions had not been extinguished by the Crown's assumption of title. In fact, Treaty 7 establishes the shared jurisdiction over navigable of the rivers: Her Majesty is bound to uphold the honour of the Crown by protecting Blackfoot navigation by water and the incidental rights of water quantity, flow and access to navigable streams.

5. Conclusion

There was no common intention to extinguish Aboriginal title to the water and waterbeds.

Even if it was possible for the Crown to unilaterally extinguish Aboriginal rights to water, Treaty 7 does not meet the test of clear and plain intent to extinguish Aboriginal water rights to water. The bundle of Aboriginal rights to water use was not extinguished under Treaty 7. In fact, Treaty 7 conferred a blanket of protection on existing Aboriginal rights to water by protecting Treaty 7 First Nations' livelihood rights, right to a reserve, and a right to navigate. Moreover, Treaty 7 First Nations' jurisdiction throughout the Treaty 7 territory was reinforced.

Treaty 7 did not extinguish Aboriginal title. None of the so-called "land cession treaties" have been examined as to whether they meet the test of extinguishment. When the tests for Treaty interpretation, as set out in *Badger* and *Marshall*, are applied, it is clear that there was no common intention to cede the land to the to give up jurisdiction over their territories. While the Crown believed that by signing treaty, Treaty 7 First Nations would forever relinquish all "their rights, titles, and privileges" to the land forever, oral history, as told by Treaty 7 Elders and written reports of the negotiations, indicates that Treaty 7 Chiefs were willing to share the fruits of the land with the Queen, but not the land itself, as it had been granted by the Creator and was not theirs to surrender. The land could not have been claimed by the prerogative power of the Crown because the Royal Proclamation required that Indian lands be ceded, collectively, willingly, to Crown at a public meeting. The Blackfoot Confederacy clearly did not cede their territory willingly, nor were they conquered. This raises the question of whether Aboriginal title has ever been extinguished.

The next step in determining what Aboriginal and treaty rights to water continue to exist, such as to give rise to a duty to consult, is examine whether subsequent legislation or Crown policy extinguished Aboriginal and Treaty rights to water in part or in whole.

CHAPTER SIX: EXTINGUISHMENT OF ABORIGINAL AND TREATY RIGHTS BY FEDERAL LEGISLATION, CROWN ACTION, OR CROWN POLICY

1. Introduction

The first step in determining the scope of the duty to consult is to identify existing Aboriginal and treaty rights. Previous chapters revealed that the Blackfoot Confederacy possessed a bundle of rights related to water including rights to navigation, rights to gather aquatic plants and medicines, rights to hunt, rights to assert jurisdiction, and rights to use water for all manner of domestic use and livelihood such as drinking, washing, tanning hides, and watering stock. This bundle of rights was further protected by the provisions in Treaty 7 that added a layer of protection to their livelihood rights. Title to the waterbeds and waters was not extinguished by consent, as there was no common intention to transfer Aboriginal title to the Crown and the Crown could not unilaterally extinguish Aboriginal title. Thus, post-treaty, Treaty 7 First Nations possessed, not only rights to water quality, quantity, and flow that enabled them continue practices, customs, and traditions involving water use, but also Aboriginal title to the waters and waterbeds throughout their territories.

Seventeen years after the conclusion of Treaty 7, the federal *North-west Irrigation Act* was passed, declaring an end to common law riparian water rights and imposing a priority licencing scheme for water users. More than half a century after the signing of Treaty 7, the Crown, assuming the federal government had jurisdiction and power to do so, transferred jurisdiction over water resources to the province. The *Natural Resources Transfer Agreement* of 1930 impacted treaty rights, both explicitly under s.12 and implicitly by establishing environmental trusts. The question to be answered is whether, in passing this legislation, Aboriginal and treaty rights were extinguished or altered in any way. Whatever rights survived the *NWIA*, the *NRTA*, and Alberta's *Water Act* are protected under s.35(1) of the constitution and trigger the duty to consult with Treaty 7 First Nations.

1.1 Extinguishment by Crown Action, Crown Policy, or Legislation

Crown policy, Crown action, or legislation may extinguish Aboriginal rights. During the colonial period the power to extinguish aboriginal rights lay with the Imperial Crown. Unless the Crown can prove that an Aboriginal or treaty right has been extinguished, Aboriginal claimants have a *prima facie* case for the existence of Aboriginal and treaty rights to water, giving rise to a duty to consult.

1.1.1 Extinguishment by Crown Policy and Crown Action

Prior to 1982 and the constitutional entrenchment of Aboriginal and treaty rights, the Crown could extinguish Aboriginal rights so long as the Crown could prove it had demonstrated a clear and plain intention to do so.

In *Adams*, the Crown attempted to prove that its "clear and plain" intention to extinguish the Aboriginal right to fish had been demonstrated by flooding the fishing area as part of process of constructing a canal. The Supreme Court rejected that argument, stating that while the action the Crown took, when read together with the Treaty "may be adequate to demonstrate a clear and plain intention in the Crown to extinguish any aboriginal title to the lands of the fishing area," it is not adequate to demonstrate a clear and plain intention to extinguish the Aboriginal right to fish.[1]

In *R. v. Nikal* it was decided that there was no exclusive Aboriginal right to fish on navigable waters because it was the Crown's policy in Western Canada not to apply the *ad medium filum aquae* presumption to navigable waters.[2] The convention or custom by which the Crown claimed title to the beds of navigable waters was based on post-contact use as a means of transportation in the fur trade. Based on this determination, the Court went concluded that the band had no proprietary right in the fishery on the river. However, extinguishment of a proprietary right to the fishery does not amount to extinguishment of the right to fish.

1.1.2 Extinguishment by Legislation

The Crown does not have to use express language to extinguish Aboriginal rights, but the legislation must be consistent in its intention to extinguish Aboriginal rights. The Crown "must demonstrate more than that, in the past, the exercise of an aboriginal right has been subject to a

---

[1] *R. v. Adams*, [1996] 3 S.C.R. 101; 138 D.L.R. (4th) 657; 202 N.R. 89; 110 C.C.C. (3d) 97; [1996] 4 C.N.L.R. 1.

[2] *R. v. Nikal*, [1996] 1 S.C.R. 1013; [1996] S.C.J. No. 47 (QL) at para 64 and following; quoting *Keewatin Power Co. v. Kenora* (1906), 13 O.L.R. 237; see also *Barthel v. Scotten* (1895), 24 Can. S.C.R. 367 and *Re Provincial Fisheries* (1896), 26 Can. S.C.R. 444.

regulatory scheme."[3] The mere "failure to recognize an aboriginal right, and the failure to grant special protection to it, do not constitute the clear and plain intention necessary to extinguish the right."[4]

To determine whether the Crown clearly or plainly intended to extinguish an Aboriginal right, regulations and legislation may be "viewed individually or as a whole." Where express language is not used, the regulatory regime must demonstrate a "consistent intention on the part of the Crown." In *Gladstone* the Court found that because the regulatory regime was inconsistent in its regulations, at times prohibiting the harvesting of herring spawn on kelp and at times encouraging Aboriginal commercial fishing. With this kind of inconsistency, the legislation cannot "be said to express a clear and plain intention to eliminate...aboriginal rights."[5]

In *Sparrow*, the Court found that the licensing provision of food fishing had not extinguished Aboriginal fishing rights because the intention of the regulation was to control the fisheries, not to deal with Indian rights. Applying the *Sparrow* test for extinguishment, the Court in *Gladstone* decided that federal fisheries regulations did not extinguish the Aboriginal right to commercial fishery. In coming to this determination, the Court took a purposive approach. It was decided that

> The government's purpose was to ensure that conservation goals were met, and that the Indian food fishery's special protection would continue; its purpose was not to eliminate aboriginal rights to fish commercially.[6]

It is clear from the case law that if the Crown can prove a clear and plain intention to extinguish Aboriginal and treaty rights, extinguishment may be effected by either legislation, Crown policy, or Crown action. Below I will consider whether the Crown could prove that the *NWIA*, *NRTA*, or the *Water Act* had extinguished Aboriginal and treaty rights to water prior to the constitutional protection afforded by s.35(1).

---

[3] *R. v. Gladstone*, [1996] 2 S.C.R. 723; [1996] S.C.J. No. 79 (QL) at para 34.
[4] *Ibid.* at para 36.
[5] *Ibid.* at para 34.
[6] *Ibid.* at para 36.

2. **Did the *North-West Irrigation Act* Extinguish Aboriginal and Treaty Rights to Water?**

The previous chapter revealed that Aboriginal rights to water not only survived the cession of title in Treaty 7, but were protected by the treaty. The previous chapter also raises a doubt as to whether Treaty 7 extinguished Aboriginal title to water and waterbeds. However, Aboriginal rights and title to water may have been subsequently extinguished by federal statute. An inquiry into the purpose of the *North-west Irrigation Act*[7] reveals that the framers had no intention of extinguishing Aboriginal rights or title to water.

The *North-west Irrigation Act* was enacted in 1894, seventeen years after the conclusion of Treaty 7, to replace common law riparian rights to water with government regulation based on a "prior appropriation" licencing scheme. All property and rights of use in any river or waterbody was, by the passage of the *Act*, vested in the Crown and a licence was required for domestic, irrigation or other purposes:

> After the passing of the Act, acquisition by riparian title or Crown grant or 'otherwise' of rights to appropriate water was barred <u>except in pursuance of an 'agreement or undertaking' existing at the time of passing of the Act</u> or in accordance with the provisions of the Act. The effect of the statute was to abrogate the common law notion that water was not the subject of ownership and the common law concept of riparian rights to water appropriation." (emphasis mine)[8]

Any Aboriginal rights and title protected by Treaty 7, being both an "agreement" and an "undertaking" existing at the time of the passage of the Act, would have survived the passage of the *North-west Irrigation Act*.

To date, there is no Canadian decision considering the effect of the *North-west Irrigation Act* on Aboriginal and treaty water rights and title. In the absence of clear and plain language in the *Act* that would extinguish Aboriginal water rights, the purpose of the Act must be considered. As held in *Gladstone*, if the government's purpose was something other than the elimination of Aboriginal rights to water, Aboriginal rights to water would not have been extinguished. If the legislation failed "to recognize an aboriginal right," or to "grant special protection to it" this does "not constitute the clear and plain intention necessary to extinguish the right."[9]

---

[7] *The North-west Irrigation Act*, S.C. 1894, c.30.

[8] Richard H. Bartlett, *Aboriginal Water Rights in Canada: A Study of Aboriginal Title to Water and Indian Water Rights*, (Calgary: Canadian Institute of Resources Law, 1988) at p.153-154.

[9] *Gladstone, supra* note 3 at para 36.

The primary purpose of the legislation was to replace the British common law riparian rights with a licencing scheme. "The debates in Parliament made no reference whatever to Indian reserves or water rights."[10] The Supreme Court has recognized that Aboriginal rights must be understood by taking into account Aboriginal legal perspectives as well as the common law, and, in fact, equal weight is to be placed on each. By replacing common law riparian rights with a legislative scheme that did not consider Aboriginal rights, Aboriginal water rights were not automatically extinguished: Aboriginal legal systems would have remained in tact.

As in other areas of the world faced with scarcity of water and a potential for water-intensive industrial or agricultural development, the doctrine of riparian rights was inadequate to the task of regulating water use. The doctrine of riparian rights, which vests water rights exclusively to riparian owners, governed the use of water, it was seen as an impediment to development on the Alberta prairies. Canada decided to vest all rights to water within the Northwest Territories in the Crown,[11] without considering whether this federal *Act* infringed the peace and order clause of the imperial 1877 treaty and the Blackfoot Confederacy's jurisdiction for beneficial use.

William Pearce of Calgary, Superintendent of Mines in charge of natural resource development, began promoting irrigation agriculture in southern Alberta in 1884. Pearce shared the view of his American colleagues that riparian rights to water were an obstacle to the economic interests of industrialists and agriculturalists. By passing federal legislation to extinguish traditional common law water rights and put in their place the right of prior appropriation, it was hoped that large-scale irrigation schemes would facilitate the development of large agrarian settlements.[12] There is no evidence in his writing and correspondence that he consulted the terms of the Indian Treaties in drafting his irrigation bill.[13]

Even if the intention to extinguish treaty protected Aboriginal rights, title, or jurisdiction had been clear, the Crown would not have had the prerogative power to unilaterally extinguish

---

[10] Bartlett, *supra* note 46 at p.155.

[11] Maureen Boyd Clark, "Water, Private Rights and the Rise of Regulation: Riparian Rights of Use in British Columbia, 1892-1939" *The Advocate* 253 at 255.

[12] Kinichi Matsui, *Reclaiming Indian Waters: Dams, Irrigation, and Indian Water Rights in Western Canada: 1858-1930*, PhD. Thesis (Vancouver: U.B.C., 2003) at 135.

[13] *Ibid.* at 139.

those rights. The test for extinguishment is not met by merely ignoring Aboriginal and Treaty rights to water. Brian Slattery argues that

> the Crown cannot exercise unilaterally any residual prerogative powers in a manner inconsistent with an historic treaty...where the Crown guarantees certain aboriginal rights in a treaty, it forfeits any asserted power to alter those rights by a unilateral prerogative act.[14]

The Crown had undertaken and promised in Treaty negotiations to protect Treaty 7 First Nations' means of livelihood, whether by traditional or modern means. The Crown specifically promised to support agricultural development on their reserves. According to Slattery, "treaty undertakings made by the Crown to aboriginal peoples give rise to particular fiduciary obligations to honour those undertakings."[15]

2.1 Early Treatment of Treaty 7 First Nations Title to Water

The water surrender agreements negotiated with the Stoneys demonstrate that the Department of Indian Affairs and hydroelectric companies recognized the rights of the Stoney people to the waterbeds and waters of the Bow River after the passage of the North-West Irrigation Act.[16] Beginning in the 1890's several hydro-electric companies sought to obtain the right to build waterpower sites on the Bow River on the Stoney Reserve. There was a legislative gap: The *NWIA* did not apply to water power and there was no clear indication that the Stoneys' treaty and Aboriginal rights had been extinguished.

Initially when the Stoneys were approached about surrendering part of their reserve for the construction of the Horseshoe Falls and Kananaskis dams, water power projects to be built on reserve, Chief John Chiniquay, the only Chief consulted, refused. The Stoneys maintained that Kananaskis Falls and Rapids were "our water powers and land"[17] and that they should receive $110,000.00 for the length of one mile of the Bow River. DIA suggested separating the cession into two parts: waterpower rights and land rights, because the officials were not sure if the river was the property of the Indians.

---

[14] Brian Slattery, Making Sense of Aboriginal and Treaty Rights" [2000] 79 Can. Bar Rev. 196 at 210.

[15] Ibid. at 211.

[16] Statutes of Canada, 1905, 4-5 Ed. 7, c.3

[17] Matsui, *supra* note 12 at 179.

The DIA asked McDougall to relay to the Stoneys that "as far as they have a proprietary interest in the water powers their interest will be fully protected by the department when these are disposed of."[18] In the end, the Stoneys agreed to surrender approximately 1,000 acres of land for the development of the Horseshoe Falls site by the Calgary Water and Transmission Company at $10 per acre; $5 per annum per capita, Chiefs and councilors to receive $25.00 per annum - payments to be made in the same manner as Treaty payments; fifty range brood mares; and $1,500 annual payment for waterpower. "The Indians also agreed to release the larger waterpower rights on the condition of receiving an additional annual five dollar per capita payment similar to what they received as Treaty 7 entitlements."[19]

The Calgary Water and Transmission Company merged with two other companies and became the Calgary Power Company led in part by none other than lawyer Richard B. Bennett. The goal of the Company was to gain control over all the power sites on the Bow River. The Company started by applying to the Interior Department for the right to develop waterpower at Kananaskis Falls. The Company held meetings with Stoneys in 1913, but the Nation refused to surrender the land unless they got a better deal: They drafted a surrender agreement similar to the previous agreement, insisting that the land and water rights belonged to them. They requested, but were unsuccessful in negotiating per capita payments upon signing, monetary compensation for surrendered land, annual per capita payments, and a rental payment of $1,500 per year, this time based on a claim of riparian rights to water.[20]

In a move that appears to have been made to circumvent the claims of Indians to Aboriginal and treaty water rights, the federal government passed the *Dominion Water Power Act* in 1919, replacing the waterpower provision in the *Dominion Lands Act*, 1908. The new Act filled the legislative gap and declared water and waterpower as national property. Under the new *Act*, Calgary Power Company applied for approval of the Ghost River water power site on the Stoney reserve in 1927. The Stoneys surrendered the land necessary and a licence was issued under the new *Act* for a term of fifty years beginning December 31, 1929. The following year the *NRTA* was passed, raising questions about provincial jurisdiction. Specifically, which department was entitled to collect rental payment on behalf of the Stoney from the Ghost

---

[18] The DIA to McDougall, 6 June 1906, RG10, vol. 3686, file 13, 119-234.

[19] Stoney Indians and chiefs to the DIA, 6 June 1906, RG10, vol.3686, file 13, 119-2,3,4.

[20] Matsui, *supra* note 12 at 189.

development: The DIA, the Department of Interior, or the province in part or in whole? In 1933 Deputy Minister of Justice issued his opinion that a "portion of the water power rental is payable to and administrable by the Dominion for the benefit of the Indians, and that the Province (although the Director of Water Resources of the Province has indicated that the Province claims the whole of the amount of such rental) has no well founded rights or claim to receive such portion of the rental."[21]

History shows that the Crown had not demonstrated a clear and plain intention to extinguish Aboriginal and treaty rights to water in passing the *North-west Irrigation Act*, and that the *Act* had no effect on Aboriginal water rights or their exercise. The federal government saw that it was necessary to pass the *Dominion Water Power Act* to facilitate the development of hydroelectricity because of the existence of Treaty 7 First Nations water rights. It remains to be considered whether Aboriginal and treaty water rights were extinguished by the transfer of jurisdiction over water from the federal crown to the province of Alberta.

3.   Did the *NRTA* Extinguish Aboriginal and Treaty Rights to Water?

The duty to consult and accommodate is grounded in the assertion of Crown sovereignty which pre-dated the *Alberta Act* and the *NRTA*. As the court stated in *Haida*, it follows that the province of Alberta, created as it was in 1905 by federal law and not by imperial act, and without a beneficial interest in the land ceded by Treaty 7, took the lands subject to the duty to consult. The lands in the province are "available to [the province] as a source of revenue whenever the estate of the Crown is disencumbered of the Indian title."[22] In *St. Catherine's Milling*, the Privy Council held that, on extinguishment of Aboriginal title, "the province would take complete title to the land."[23] As has been argued in the previous chapter, Aboriginal title to the waterbeds and waters of the province could not have been extinguished by Treaty 7 because there was no common intent to extinguish Aboriginal title. To the extent that there is some form of sui generis proprietary interest, Aboriginal title, or environmental trust in the waters in the province of Alberta, the province's jurisdiction must be exercised subject to that interest or trust.

---

[21]   W. Stuart Edwards for H.H Rowat, 19 July 1933, RG 10, vol. 8057, file 772/32-3-3, pt. 3.

[22]   *Haida Nation* v. *British Columbia (Minister of Forests)*, [2004] 3 S.C.R. 511; [2004] S.C.J. No. 70 (Q.L.); 2004 SCC 73 at para 59; *St. Catherine's Milling and Lumber Co. v. The Queen* (1888), 14 App. Cas. 46 (P.C.).

[23]   *Delgamu'ukw* v. *British Columbia*, [1997] S.C.J. No. 108 (QL); [1997] 3 S.C.R. 1010 at para. 175; *St. Catherine's Milling and Lumber, supra* note 22.

The *NRTA* did not extinguish any treaty-protected Aboriginal rights. Rather, the *NRTA* adds another layer of protection over Indian hunting, fishing, and trapping, and rights incidental thereto to water quality, quantity and flow sufficient to support fishing and hunting on Crown lands and lands to which they have a right of access. The *NRTA* created a corresponding duty for the province to ensure that sufficient resources remain to support the Indian traditional livelihood to protect an environment conducive to maintaining wildlife populations.

3.1 Principles for Interpreting the *NRTA*

The degree of consultation required may be influenced by the historical context of the relationship between the Crown and First Nations. It has been suggested that "[u]nderstanding the historical relationship between the Crown and Aboriginals is a necessary precondition to conceptualizing reconciliation and articulating what reconciliation demands."[24] The negotiations leading up to the finalization of the *NRTA* was a turning point in the on-going historical relationship between the Crown and First Nations. In *Blais*,[25] the Court stated that an analysis of livelihood rights under the *NRTA* "must be anchored in the historical context of the provision."[26]

Interpretation of constitutional guarantees further requires a purposive approach. The Supreme Court, in *Blais*, referred to the principles of interpretation set out in *Big M Drug Mart*:

> it is important not to overshoot the actual purpose of the right or freedom in question, but to recall that the [constitutional provision] was not enacted in a vacuum, and must therefore ... be placed in its proper linguistic, philosophic and historical contexts.[27]

The rules of legislative and constitutional interpretation require a purposive approach. In *Big M Drugmart*, the Supreme Court stated that "[a]n understanding of the scheme of that Act and its basic purpose and effect is integral to any analysis of its constitutional validity.[28]

---

[24] Michael Hudson, "Reconciling Diversity with Unity: Canadian Federalism in the 21st Century" unpublished paper presented to the Canadian Bar Association Canadian Legal Conference in Vancouver, August 14-16, 2005.

[25] The Supreme Court in *R. v. Blais*, [2003] 2 S.C.R. 236; [2003] S.C.J. No. 44; 2003 SCC 44, considered whether Metis were Indians such that their rights were protected by the NRTA.

[26] Frank Tough argues, the Court has "not encountered a grounded historical analysis in respect of the effect of the *Natural Resources Transfer Agreement* on treaty rights." He points out that the wording of the provision addressing Treaty rights in the NRTA is cited by the Courts "mechanically and completely without historical depth:" Frank J. Tough, "The Forgotten Constitution: The Natural Resources Transfer Agreements and Indian Livelihood Rights, CA. 1925-1933" 2004 41 Alta. L. Rev. 999 at 1000 [hereinafter "Tough"].

[27] *Blais*, *supra* note 25 at para 17 quoting *R. v. Big M Drug Mart Ltd.*, [1985] S.C.J. No. 17; [1985] 1 S.C.R. 295 at p. 344.

> [E]ither an unconstitutional purpose or an unconstitutional effect can invalidate legislation. *All legislation is animated by an object the legislature intends to achieve. This object is realized through the impact produced by the operation and application of the legislation.* Purpose and effect respectively, in the sense of the legislation's object and its ultimate impact, are clearly linked, if not indivisible. Intended and actual effects have often been looked to for guidance in assessing the legislation's object and thus, its validity…Moreover, *consideration of the object of legislation is vital if rights are to be fully protected.*[29]

Thus an analysis of the objectives of the *NRTA* and the impact that it has had on Aboriginal and Treaty rights is necessary to protect those rights that pre-existed the *NRTA*.

The purposive approach to interpreting constitutional documents was again extolled by Supreme Court in *Van der Peet*:

> because constitutions are, by their very nature, documents aimed at a country's future as well as its present; the Constitution must be interpreted in a manner which renders it "capable of growth and development over time to meet new social, political and historical realities often unimagined by its framers": Hunter, supra, at p. 155.[30]

The first step in the analysis, therefore, is to ascertain the purpose of the *NRTA*. To do so, it is necessary to make a detailed historical inquiry into the events and ideas leading to the final draft of the provisions affecting Indians and Indian rights.[31]

3.1.1   The Purpose of *NRTA* s.12

Section 12 of the *Natural Resources Transfer Agreement* (*NRTA*) addresses the status of the right to hunt, trap and fish following the transfer of unoccupied Crown lands from Canada to the Province.

> In order to secure to the Indians of the Province the continuance of the supply of game and fish for their support and subsistence, Canada agrees that the law respecting game in force in the Province from time to time shall apply to the Indians within the boundaries thereof, provided, however, that the said Indians shall have the right, which the Province hereby assures to them, of hunting, trapping and fishing game and fish for food at all

---

[28] *Big M Drug Mart, supra* note 27 at para 5.

[29] *Ibid.* at para 80-81.

[30] *R. v. Van der Peet*, [1996] S.C.J. No. 77, [1996] 2 S.C.R. 507 at para 21.

[31] I have relied heavily on the meticulous historical research of Dr. Frank Tough. All further references to historical documents in this chapter appear in his various published and unpublished works on this topic. He may or may not agree with my legal arguments.

seasons of the year on all unoccupied Crown lands or on any other lands to which the said Indians may have a right of access.[32]

The over-arching purpose of the *NRTA* was "to put the provinces of Alberta, Manitoba and Saskatchewan on an equal footing with the other Canadian provinces by giving them jurisdiction over and ownership of their natural resources."[33] The *NRTA* transferred all the lands and minerals from the federal Crown to the province subject to any existing trusts. Chapter 5 established that Treaty 7 First Nations have existing *sui generis* proprietary or other rights to the waters of the province by virtue of the Treaty. Furthermore, Treaty 7 First Nations' rights to a healthy aquatic environment may be "incidental rights" meaningfully linked with their hunting, fishing, and trapping rights. These rights constitute "trusts" or "interests" limiting provincial jurisdiction with regard to conduct affecting the aquatic environment.

The Government of Alberta, in its Consultation Guidelines, recognizes First Nations rights respecting public lands as provided for in the Treaties and the Natural Resources Transfer Agreement, including the rights to hunt, fish, and trap for food.[34] Clearly the Alberta government has knowledge of the existence of Aboriginal rights, and is aware of the corresponding duty to consult with First Nations regarding any conduct contemplated by the province that might adversely affect those rights.

Despite acknowledgement by the province of the existence of hunting, trapping, and fishing rights, it remains necessary to determine the scope of the duty to consult pursuant to rights protected under the *NRTA*. The factors to be considered are 1) the strength of the case supporting the existence of the right or title; and 2) the seriousness of the potentially adverse effect upon the right or title claimed.

The overall purpose of the *NRTA* was to transfer natural resources from the jurisdiction of the Dominion government to the provinces. The motivation for doing so was simple economics. The prairie provinces wanted the same opportunities as the other provinces for development and profit from the wealth of natural resources within their respective borders. The Department of Indian Affairs was primarily concerned with the protection of Indian livelihood rights from

---

[32] *Constitution Act*, 1930, 20-21 George V, c. 26 (U.K.), Schedule 1.

[33] *Blais, supra* note 25 at para 10.

[34] Alberta Environment, "First Nation Consultation Guidelines (Regulatory Authorizations and Environmental Impact Assessments) Draft 1, May 18, 2006" accessed at
http://www.aand.gov.ab.ca/AANDFlash/Files/AENV_FN_Guidelines_Draft_1_May_18_2006.pdf, on July 31, 2006.

encroachment by non-Indian trappers. The Hudson's Bay Company, while not a party, was concerned about protecting trapping as a commercial industry as well as any rights the Company may have to the fishery.

At the early stages of negotiation, Duncan Campbell Scott, Deputy Superintendent General of Indian Affairs advocated for "hunting and fishing reserves and for exemptions in favour of Indians who are hunting and fishing purely for their own sustenance."[35] His concern was that provincial authority to enact game regulations would negatively affect Indian hunting.

Lieutenant-Colonel O. M. Biggar, K.C., counsel for the Dominion was not in agreement. He pointed out that "[i]n southern Alberta the Indians have become agriculturists and have ceased to depend for their livelihood on hunting, but this is by no means the case in the north, where many of the bands depend upon trapping and fishing for a livelihood."[36] By 'livelihood' Biggar clearly meant to include commercial trapping, and fishing: Trapping an inherently commercial activity. It was the dependence on commercial trade in fish and game of the northern Indians that motivated Dominion officials to consider the protection of livelihood rights from encroachment by the province. It appears that the Treaty rights of Treaty 7 First Nations were not given a great deal of consideration. Nonetheless, Treaty 7 First Nations benefited from the protections that were ultimately afforded all Indians of the province under the *NRTA*.

The Department of Indian Affairs was motivated in large part by the concern that the province would not adequately protect game populations. Biggar explained:

> The Department of Indian Affairs is just as much, or even more concerned to secure the preservation of game…In the old days the Indians themselves took care to conserve and protect the game so as to yield them their livelihood as readily as possible, and they were in effect the only trappers. Now, however, the commercial trappers show no such concern…notwithstanding the game laws, they should be allowed to hunt and fish out of season for their own food.[37]

The framers of s.12 could not agree to the wording for the protection of Indian hunting. Biggar felt that hunting "should be limited to continuing to the Indians the same rights in unoccupied Crown lands after their transfer to the Province as they now enjoy in respect of

---

[35] Memorandum, Scott (29 January 1925), Ottawa, NAC (RG 10, vol. 6820, file 492-4-2, pt.11) in Tough, *supra* note 26 at p.1019.

[36] Memorandum, Biggar (30 January 1925), Ottawa, NAC (RG 10, vol. 6820, file 492-4-2, pt. 1) in Tough, *supra* note 26 at p 1020.

[37] Ibid.

them."[38] Indian Affairs solicitor A.S. Williams advocated that Indians should be immune from provincial game laws based on federal jurisdiction over Indians and Indian lands.

Clearly the primary purpose of the *NRTA* s. 12 was to protect the traditional livelihood of First Nations. In the final version, hunting, fishing, and trapping were included as means of obtaining subsistence. Where the Indian hunting and fishing right had been "freely and fully" exercisable under the 1926 version, it was restricted "for food" under the 1930 Agreement. Closed seasons would not affect hunting and fishing as the wording "at all seasons of the year" was included. The geographical territory was expanded to include unoccupied Crown land as well as "any lands to which the said Indians may have a right of access."[39]

The framers of the *NRTA* s. 12 intended to protect fish and game populations. The preambular phrase, "In order to secure to the Indians of the Province the continuance of the supply of game and fish for their support and subsistence" placed an obligation on the province to pass laws that would support the continuing supply of game and fish for Indian subsistence. Tough argues that "the province acquired the obligation to ensure through conservation that the resources existed in order to secure a supply of game and fish to the Indians."[40] If such is the case, any time the province contemplates conduct that would adversely affect the environment supporting Indian hunting, fishing, and trapping, the province would not only be under a duty to consult, but would also be in breach of its obligations under the *NRTA*.

3.1.2 The Effect of the *NRTA* on Treaty 7 First Nations' Water Rights

The second stage of inquiry into the meaning of constitutional documents is an analysis of their effect. Section 12 of the *NRTA* has been held to have significantly altered the nature and scope of Treaty rights in the Province of Alberta: The *NRTA* created an environmental trust responsibility of the provincial Crown, expanded the exercise of Treaty rights geographically, added the right to fish and trap, and limited the right to hunt and fish "for food."

---

[38] Memorandum, Biggar to Scott (12 February 1925), Ottawa, NAC (RG 10, ibid.) in Tough, *supra* note 26 at 1021 to 1022.

[39] Frank Tough points out that the protection of Indian hunting and fishing rights were not achieved "by arguing for the exchange of some rights for other rights." Tough, *supra* note 26 at 1036.

[40] Tough, *supra* note 26.

3.1.2.1 Creation of Trust Obligations

The *Alberta Act*,[41] had provided that the Crown's interest waters in Alberta, under the *Northwest Irrigation Act*, 1898, would "continue to be vested in the Crown and administered by the Government of Canada for the purposes of Canada."[42] The federal Crown retained jurisdiction over the lands and waters of the province until the Western provinces took jurisdiction over the lands and resources through the *NRTA* in 1930. The province took jurisdiction subject to existing interests and trusts. "[T]he interest of the Crown in all Crown lands" including all "lands, mines, minerals or royalties" would thereafter "belong to the Province, subject to any trusts existing in respect thereof, and to any interest other than that of the Crown in the same." Furthermore, "the said lands, mines, minerals and royalties [were to] be administered by the Province."[43]

The province covenanted to maintain the Crown's obligations and to

> carry out in accordance with the terms thereof …every other arrangement whereby any person has become entitled to any interest [in land] as against the Crown, and further agrees not to affect or alter any term of any such … other arrangement by legislation or otherwise, except either with the consent of all the parties thereto other than Canada or in so far as any legislation may apply generally to all similar agreements relating to lands, mines or minerals in the Province or to interests therein, irrespective of who may be the parties thereto.[44]

The Natural Resources Transfer Agreements were largely concerned with the transfer of contractual and related liabilities from Canada to the provinces. The *NRTA* was not a grant of title, but an administrative transfer of the responsibilities, including obligations to "the Indians within the boundaries" of the Province.[45] The historical record reveals that the drafters did not turn their minds to the possibility that First Nations may have interests in the land and waters of the province, other than for unfulfilled Treaty promises to a reserve. It could be argued that implied rights to water under Treaty 7 constitute "other arrangements" for the purposes of s.2. If that is the case, the province would have no power to "affect or alter any term of any such … other arrangement by legislation or otherwise."

---

[41] *Alberta Act*, 4-5 Edward VII, c. 3 (Canada), [Assented to 20th July, 1905].

[42] *Constitution Act*, 1930, 20-21 George V, c. 26 (U.K.), Schedule 1, commonly referred to as the *Natural Resources Transfer Agreement*.

[43] *NRTA, supra* note 42 at para 1.

[44] *NRTA, supra* note 42 para 2

[45] *Blais, supra* note 25 at para 19.

If Treaty 7 First Nations have unextinguished rights to water, the *Water Act*'s priority licencing system, combined with Treaty 7 and the *NRTA*, which provided that "the interest of the Crown in all Crown lands...shall belong to the Province *subject to any trusts* existing in respect thereof, and to any interest other than that of the Crown," results in the priority and protection of Treaty 7 First Nations' rights to water. While there is no Canadian jurisprudence yet on this point, American case law has established that the date of reservation of water rights on an Indian reserve for irrigation was the date of the establishment of the reserve.[46] An early priority date will require other water rights holders to take water subject to Indian water rights. The *Water Act* has capped the date of priority at 1894. It would appear that riparian rights holders predating 1894, which includes Treaty 7 First Nations, have priority water rights.

3.1.2.2 Geographical Expansion

Writing for the Supreme Court of Canada in *Badger*, Cory J. described the *NRTA* as having had "the clear intention of both limiting and expanding the treaty right to hunt." Traditional livelihood rights were reduced by being expressly limited "for food" as opposed to commercial purposes. The geographic scope of the right was expanded, no longer being confined to "the tract surrendered" but extending to all unoccupied Crown lands throughout the Province and any other lands to which Indians have a right of access."

Supreme Court of Canada cases such as *R. v. Horseman*[47] and *Badger*[48] dealing with the effect of the *NRTA* on Treaty rights in Alberta have arisen in the context of Treaty 8. The same analysis would apply to Treaty 7, with one notable exception: the *NRTA* appears to result in a further expansion of Treaty rights in the context of Treaty 7, insofar as it assures the right to hunt, fish, and trap. Treaty 7 does not refer to fishing and trapping - only to the right of Indians "to pursue their avocations of hunting," presumably because the Blackfoot considered the consumption of fish to be taboo and they were not typically commercial trappers. Under the *NRTA*, Treaty 7 First Nations have the additional right to fish and trap in the Treaty area as well

---

[46] *Winters v. United States*, 207 U.S. 564 (1908), 52 L.Ed. 340 aff'g 143 F.740 (9th Cir. 1906). A representative of AENV stated that the American system is based on a system of prior appropriation while Alberta's system is based on prior allocation. The implication is that First Nations, not having an allocation, would have no prior right to water. This position is not supported by historical legal opinion, see quote by Challies.

[47] *R. v. Horseman*, [1990] S.C.J. No. 39 (QL); [1990] 1 S.C.R. 901.

[48] *R. v. Badger*, [1996] 1 S.C.R. 771; [1996] S.C.J. No. 39 (QL).

as on all unoccupied Crown lands and other lands to which they have a right of access. In addition, they have rights incidental to rights to hunt, trap, and fish.

In the *Horseman* case, the Supreme Court considered whether Indian hunting rights included the right to hunt commercially. It was determined that, as a result of the *NRTA* s.12, Indian hunting rights were restricted to subsistence while being expanded to include the entire province. Cory J., writing for the majority, rejected the appellants arguments that the passage of the *NRTA* required the approval or consent of First Nations prior to reducing or abridging Treaty livelihood rights, and that a unilateral change to and derogation of Treaty rights would bring dishonour to the Crown. The Court also rejected the argument that "the Crown should be looked upon as a trustee of the Native hunting rights."[49] *Horseman* has directed a long line of cases that appear to restrict Indian hunting.

The doctrine of Parliamentary sovereignty allowed Treaty and Aboriginal rights to be unilaterally altered by statute passed by a competent legislature, "in the absence of constitutional barriers such as those embodied in the *Royal Proclamation of 1763* and s.35(1) of the *Constitution Act, 1982*."[50] This doctrine, apart from the historical record of negotiations, appears to have influenced the Court in its decision in *R. v. Horseman*. In that case, the appellant had argued that the *NRTA* "was meant to protect the rights of Indians and not to derogate from those rights."[51] The Court rejected this argument, relying on Dickson J.'s decisions in *Frank* v. *The Queen*; *R.* v. *Sutherland,* and *Moosehunter* v. *The Queen*.[52] The Court stated that "[i]t is also clear that the Transfer Agreements were meant to modify the division of powers originally set out in the Constitution Act, 1867 (formerly the British North America Act, 1867)."[53] In exchange for the restriction of Indian hunting to food only, "[t]he geographical areas in which the Indian people could hunt was widely extended."[54]

---

[49] *Horseman, supra* note 47 at para 57.

[50] Brian Slattery, Making Sense of Aboriginal and Treaty Rights" [2000] 79 Can. Bar Rev. 196 at 204.

[51] *Horseman, supra* note 47 at para 57.

[52] *Frank* v. *The Queen*, [1978] 1 S.C.R. 95; *R.* v. *Sutherland*, [1980] 2 S.C.R. 451; *Moosehunter* v. *The Queen*, [1981] 1 S.C.R. 282.

[53] *Horseman, supra* note 47 at para 59.

[54] *Ibid.* at para 60.

The test for extinguishment, as set out in *R. v. Sparrow*, "is that the Sovereign's intention must be clear and plain if it is to extinguish an aboriginal right."[55] In *R. v. Badger*, Mr. Justice Cory, for the majority of the Supreme court, made it clear that the same 'clear and plain' test applied to the unilateral extinguishment of a Treaty right:

> ...the onus of proving that a treaty or aboriginal right has been extinguished lies upon the Crown. There must be "strict proof of the fact of extinguishment" and evidence of a clear and plain intention on the part of the government to extinguish treaty rights.

The majority concluded that, although the *Natural Resources Transfer Agreement* did not entirely extinguish and replace all Treaty hunting rights, it extinguished commercial hunting rights and otherwise altered the exercise of hunting rights. The language that effectively extinguished commercial hunting rights

> did not make express reference to such a right, nor was it shown that the Crown made any acknowledgement of the right's existence...Nevertheless the statement that Indians would be required to abide by the game laws of the Province, combined with the omission of any reference to rights to hunt for purposes other than food, was, in the Supreme Court's view, a sufficient basis to conclude that the clear and plain standard had been met.[56]

The Supreme Court in *R. v. Gladstone* explained the reasoning in *Badger*:

> Section 12 of the Natural Resources Transfer Agreement (*NRTA*)... is a provision in a constitutional document, the enactment of which provides for a permanent settlement of the legal rights of the aboriginal groups to whom it applies...The *NRTA* was aimed at achieving a permanent clarification of the province's legislative jurisdiction and of the legal rights of aboriginal peoples within the province...[T]he *NRTA* can be seen as evincing the necessary clear and plain intention to extinguish aboriginal rights to hunt commercially in the province to which it applies...[57]

This interpretation of the purpose of the *NRTA* seems to be at odds with the historical record. As discussed above, the Department of Indian Affairs had specifically set out to protect existing Indian interests in hunting and fishing for commercial purposes against encroachment of white trappers because they feared that the provinces would not. To a certain extent the intended purpose of the drafters of the provision were met in that "[b]oth the area of hunting and the way in which the hunting could be conducted was extended and removed from the jurisdiction of

---

[55] *R. v. Sparrow*, [1990] 1 S.C.R. 1075; [1990] S.C.J. No. 49 at para 37.

[56] Kenneth J. Tyler, "The Division of Powers and Aboriginal Water Rights Issues": National Symposium on Water Law, Environmental Law CLE Programme, 1999, unpublished at 55.

[57] *R. v. Gladstone*, [1996] 2 S.C.R. 723; [1996] S.C.J. No. 79 (QL) at para 38.

provincial governments."⁵⁸ The historical record is silent as to why "for food" was included in the final draft, but it does not appear from the historical record that there was any intention to expand the geographical right in exchange for restrictions on commercial hunting and fishing rights.

The inclusion of the right to fish, combined with the geographical expansion of fishing, hunting, and trapping rights means that Treaty 7 First Nations have a right to fish on all lakes and watercourses within the province to the extent that they are "lands to which they have a right of access." The expansion of Treaty 7 livelihood rights, coupled with a positive duty to protect environmental resources that support Indian livelihood rights, leads to extended environmental rights: Any conduct by the province, such as authorizations under the *Water Act* to pollute, divert, or otherwise adversely affect Treaty 7 First Nations' hunting, fishing, and trapping rights under the *NRTA* would trigger the duty to consult. The end result is that First Nations of the entire province must be consulted on all matters affecting the environment throughout the province, not merely within their traditional territories. The question then becomes one of how to determine whether a First Nation is "directly affected" as defined by the *Water Act*. Alberta's answer has been to chart the traditional land use areas of First Nations and to only consult on developments within those areas. However, this does not address the geographical expansion of Treaty 7 First Nations' rights which extend far beyond their traditional land use areas.

3.1.2.3 Incidental Rights

Certain activities related to hunting, fishing, and trapping, protected under the *NRTA*, may be rights incidental to protected livelihood rights.

Simon and *Sundown* set the test to determine whether certain <u>activities</u> are reasonably incidental to the right to hunt, trap or fish. In *Sundown* the Court applied the reasonable person standard to define what rights are "reasonably incidental" to livelihood rights. The standard of reasonableness is that of the reasonable person who is dispassionate, "fully apprised of the circumstances of the treaty rights holder," and aware of the manner of hunting and fishing at the time of Treaty.⁵⁹

---

⁵⁸ *Horseman, supra* note 47 at para 60.
⁵⁹ *R. v. Sundown*, [1999] 1 S.C.R. 393; [1999] S.C.J. No.13 (QL) at para 28-30 at para 29.

To be effective, a right must embody those activities reasonably incidental to the act of hunting itself. A right reasonably incidental to a treaty right to hunt, will be ascertained using a factual and historical inquiry. The right will be "significantly connected" to "an actual practiced treaty right." It will include activities that are not only "essential, or integral" but will include, more broadly, "activities which are meaningfully related or linked."[60]

While *Simon* and *Sundown* dealt with the rights of Indians to participate in reasonably incidental activities, rights to the protection of resources and the environment may also be reasonably incidental to the right to hunt, trap, and fish. The hypothetical reasonable man would likely conclude there is no substance to rights to hunt, trap, and fish unless there are animals or fish and the habitat to support them. Section 12 of the *NRTA* was intended "to secure to the Indians of the Province the continuance of the supply of game and fish for their support and subsistence." This suggests that the province has the corresponding duty to ensure a supply of healthy fish and game sufficient to support Indian traditional livelihood needs.

The Court has not gone so far as to mandate the province to pass conservation laws to protect Treaty rights. However, the Court recognized in Sundown that "[i]n many, if not most, situations, the conservation of fish and game requires the preservation of their habitat."[61] *Badger* and *Sundown* held that "both Treaty No. 8 and the *NRTA* specifically provided that hunting rights would be subject to regulation pertaining to conservation."

> [B]y the terms of both the Treaty and the NRTA, provincial game laws would be applicable to Indians so long as they were aimed at conserving the supply of game. However, the provincial government's regulatory authority under the Treaty and the NRTA did not extend beyond the realm of conservation.[62]

It is well settled that provincial laws could only restrict treaty hunting and fishing rights so long as they related to conservation and only to the extent that they could be justified under the *Sparrow* test. In *Claxton v. Saanichton Marina Ltd.*, a treaty case in British Columbia where there was no equivalent of the *NRTA* s.12, the Court acknowledged that a healthy habitat is required for the exercise of the right to fish. The B.C. Court of Appeal held that the Treaty right to a fishery "meant not only the right to catch fish but also the place where the right can be exercised." The court further stated that the right to the fishery does "not amount to a proprietary

---

[60] *Ibid.* at para 28-30.
[61] *Ibid.* at para 38.
[62] Badger, supra note 48 at para 70.

interest in the sea bed nor a contractual right to a fishing ground." Nonetheless, "it protects the Indians against infringement of their right to carry on the fishery as formerly. This includes the right to travel to and from the fishery." The construction of a marina would "derogate from the right of Indians to carry on their fisheries as formerly in the area protected by treaty." It would "impede their right of access to an important area of the bay" and "destroy an aquatic habitat." Having determined that the development would have a "harmful impact on the right of fishing granted by the treaty," the Court granted declaratory relief.[63]

To exercise the right to fish, First Nations must have, not only the incidental right to access waters, but also a right to quality, quantity and flow of water sufficient "to secure to the Indians of the Province the continuance of the supply of game and fish for their support and subsistence." The environmental rights of First Nations and the corresponding positive duty to conserve the aquatic eco-system are "meaningfully related or linked." Moreoever, they are in keeping with the provision in the *NRTA* and the spirit and intent of Treaty 7 which protects the livelihood of First Nations. The positive duty on the Crown to pass legislation protecting water quality, quantity, and flow and to otherwise manage natural resources is a necessary aspect reconciling the British common law with Aboriginal legal perspectives and triggers the duty to consult.

Arguably, the right to water quality, quantity, and flow is a right incidental to the exercise of livelihood rights protected by the *NRTA*. In the alternative, Treaty 7 First Nations have an incidental right to engage in activities that would ensure that a healthy aquatic environment is maintained to enable them to exercise their livelihood rights under the *NRTA*. The *NRTA* mandates the province to conserve water resources to support Indian subsistence, and, thereby giving rise to the duty to consult with Treaty 7 First Nations regarding water allocation and use, and any development affecting the waters in the province.

3.1.2.4 Lands to Which Indians Have a Right of Access

The geographical expansion of Treaty hunting, fishing, and trapping rights is limited to unoccupied Crown lands. Although the province may have a duty to protect the environment, the wording of the *NRTA* suggests that this duty is restricted to unoccupied Crown lands to which Indians have a right of access. Where Indians have a right of access to Crown lands, the exercise

---

[63] *Claxton v. Saanichton Marina Ltd.*, [1989] 3 C.N.L.R. 46.

of the Treaty right must be compatible with the Crown's use of the land.[64] The measure of incompatibility with the Crown's occupancy is whether the exercise of the right is not only "contrary to the purpose underlying that occupancy", but it "prevent[s] the realization of that purpose."[65] If the exercise of the right to fish was "wholly incompatible" with the Crown's use of the land and appurtenant waters, use of the waters for fishing or other purposes would be disallowed and any rights in the water would be extinguished.[66]

Any existing Treaty rights to water are further restricted to lands not "required or taken up for settlement or for any other purpose."[67] Although Indians do not have a right to access to lands once they are "taken up," *Mikisew* suggests that the Crown has a duty to consult with First Nations prior to "taking up" lands. With the exercise of certain Treaty rights, such as the right to hunt, it is difficult to conceive of the waters being taken up by the Crown for a purpose that would be wholly incompatible with the exercise of the Treaty right to water. While the province may argue that the *Northwest Irrigation Act* was as a "taking up" of lands, this argument cannot succeed. The *Act* gave jurisdiction over water to the Crown and replaced common law riparian rights with a regime structured around the doctrine of prior appropriation. It did not preclude Indians from fishing, hunting, or trapping on waters in the province, as the exercise of their livelihood rights was not "wholly incompatible" with the purpose of the Act.

4. Were Aboriginal and treaty rights extinguished by the *Water Resources Act* or the *Water Act*?

After Alberta received jurisdiction over water, the province passed various pieces of legislation leading up to the *Water Resources Act*,[68] replacing the federal *North-west Irrigation Act* in regulating water use, and continuing the priority licencing scheme. The *Water Act*, 2000 replaced the *Water Resources Act*, but maintained the licencing scheme. The province of Alberta is constitutionally incapable of extinguishing an Aboriginal right:

> Since 1871, the exclusive power to legislate in relation to "Indians, and Lands reserved for the Indians" has been vested with the federal government by virtue of s.91(24) of the

---

[64] *Sundown, supra* note 59 at para 39.

[65] R. v. *Sioui*; 1990 CarswellQue 103; [1990] 1 S.C.R. 1025, 109 N.R. 22, 56 C.C.C. (3d) 225, 70 D.L.R. (4th) 427, [1990] 3 C.N.L.R. 127 at p. 1073

[66] *Sundown, supra* note 59 at para 40.

[67] *Ibid.* at para 42.

[68] *Water Resources Act*, R.S.A., 1980, c.W-5.

Constitution Act, 1867. That head of jurisdiction, in my opinion, encompasses within it the exclusive power to extinguish aboriginal rights, including aboriginal title.[69]

The *Water Act* of Alberta and its precursors do not address Aboriginal water rights, but even if they did, the province of Alberta has no power to extinguish existing Aboriginal rights.

5. Conclusion

The *North-west Irrigation Act* did not clearly or plainly extinguish treaty-protected Aboriginal rights to water. Mere regulation does not extinguish Aboriginal rights. Treaty 7 First Nations continued to possess Aboriginal and treaty rights unrestricted by the *North-west Irrigation Act*, the only purpose of which was to impose a licencing scheme on water use. Indeed, crown action and crown policy reinforces the proposition that Treaty 7 First Nations had continuing rights to water after Treaty 7 was negotiated: The Crown say fit to negotiate an additional treaty with the Stoneys relating to the use of the Bow River for hydro-electric power.

Assuming the federal crown had the power to transfer jurisdiction over water to the province without the consent of First Nations where treaties had been negotiated, the purpose and effect of the *NRTA* was not to extinguish Aboriginal or treaty rights. If anything, the *NRTA* added yet another blanket of protection over treaty-protected Aboriginal rights. The Crown has interpreted the legislative protection promised in Treaty negotiations and reinforced by *NRTA* s.12 as a limitation to the Treaty right to hunt, fish, and trap. Treaty 7 First Nations had been guaranteed the right to hunt under Treaty. Under the *NRTA* their right to hunt was expanded to include fishing and trapping rights. The *NRTA* may have actually expanded livelihood rights to include incidental rights to the quality, quantity and flow of water sufficient to support their livelihood by trapping and fishing. To the extent that Treaty 7 First Nations have unextinguished *sui generis* proprietary interest or a Treaty arrangement for the use of water, the exercise of provincial jurisdiction may be subject to these interests and arrangements.

I have argued in this chapter that recent developments in consultation law may be applied to Indian hunting, trapping, and fishing rights under the *NRTA* s.12. While the Court may have rejected the duty to consult with Treaty First Nations prior to the finalization of the *NRTA*,[70] s.35(1) of the Constitution now mandates consultation whenever there is a *prima facie* case for

---

[69] *Delgamu'ukw* v. *British Columbia*, [1997] S.C.J. No. 108 (QL); [1997] 3 S.C.R. 1010 at para 37.
[70] *Horseman, supra* note 47.

the existence of an Aboriginal or Treaty right and the province contemplated conduct that will adversely impact those rights. The province of Alberta has recently developed its consultation policies in acknowledgement of its duty to consult regarding impacts on First Nations' rights under the *NRTA*.

Rights to water quality, quantity and flow, and access to water are incidental to the right to hunt, trap and fish. Arguably, if there is a poor aquatic environment, animal populations will be depleted resulting in an inability to fish for food.[71] Although the right to fish does not appear in the Treaty, Treaty 7 First Nations nevertheless have a right to fish for food pursuant to s.12 of the *NRTA*. Any negative impact on the aquatic environment <u>anywhere in the province</u> that might deplete or contaminate fish stocks would be an infringement of the right to fish for food. Thus the *NRTA* has potentially expanded Treaty 7 First Nations' right to water to extend throughout the province.

All that is required to trigger the duty to consult is a prima facie case for the existence of an Aboriginal right. It is evident from the analysis of the various means of extinguishment that Aboriginal rights to water have not been extinguished by Treaty 7, Crown policy and action, the *Northwest Irrigation Act* or the *Water Act*. A prima facie case having been made out, the province has a duty to consult, the exact scope of that duty depending on the potential seriousness of the adverse effect on the Aboriginal right claimed.

---

[71] *Halfway River First Nation* v. *B.C. (Ministry of Forests)*, [1999] 4 C.N.L.R. 1 para 144 (emphasis in the original) per Finch J.A.

CHAPTER SEVEN: CONCLUSION
Purpose of this book:

This book answers the question of whether Treaty 7 First Nations have a prima facie case for a claim to Aboriginal or Treaty rights to water so as to trigger a duty to consult with them regarding water management, and whether Alberta's consultation policy and Water for Life Strategy satisfy the duty to consult. I have concluded that not only did Treaty 7 and subsequent legislation not extinguish Aboriginal rights and title to water and waterbeds, but that Treaty 7 and the *NRTA* added a layer of protection over existing Aboriginal rights. Section 52 of the Constitution and the principles of constitutionalism and rule of law require that all government policy and action is consistent with the s.35(1) protection of Aboriginal and treaty rights. Thus the province has a duty to engage in "deep consultation" with Treaty 7 First Nations, especially regarding treaty-protected and NRTA-protected Aboriginal rights.

Alberta's consultation policy

Alberta's consultation policy fails to recognize any proprietary rights to water and any jurisdiction over water. The Water for Life policy treats First Nations as "stakeholders" with no priority over other stakeholders such as industry, agriculturalists, or municipalities. Likewise, Alberta's consultation policy only recognizes traditional uses of the land and fails to protect Aboriginal and treaty rights in their full force and vigour. These policies fail to recognize and protect the unique relationship of Treaty 7 First Nations with the Crown. The Supreme Court in *Mikisew* held that consultation and accommodation are processes that reconcile the Crown's assertion of sovereignty with the prior occupation of First Nations. Engaging in consultation and making efforts to accommodate First Nations interests, are part of the process of managing the treaty relationship. Alberta's consultation policy is inconsistent with protection of existing Aboriginal and treaty rights under s.35(1) and is therefore void.

Reconciliation and consultation

The overarching purpose of consultation with First Nations on matters relating to resource use and management is reconciliation. Reconciliation is a processes that is never concluded: It is an on-going relationship arising from the Constitutional guarantee of Aboriginal rights, the assertion of Crown sovereignty over the lands and resources of Aboriginal peoples, and the honor of the Crown.

The Supreme Court has not consistently defined the process of reconciliation: The characterization has ranged from a "balancing of interests" approach to "managing the treaty relationship." Alberta has chosen to use the balancing of interests approach in developing its consultation policy, placing societal economic needs, interests, and ambitions on par with Aboriginal and treaty rights. True reconciliation must take into account Aboriginal laws and perspectives. By circumventing the Crown's historical relationship with First Nations, devolving responsibility for consultation to proponents, and focusing on balancing the economic interests of industrialists, agriculturalist, and municipalities with the Aboriginal and treaty rights of Treaty 7 First Nations, the province has exploited Treaty 7 First Nations and deprived them of the exercise of their rights to water and water use.

WPACs represent an opportunity to assert Treaty 7 First Nations' jurisdiction and share governance of the watershed in a way that reconciles Aboriginal interests, legal systems, and cultures with the assertion of Crown sovereignty and other competing interests. However, so long as the balancing of interests approach is the framework being used in a power-imbalanced environment, Treaty 7 First Nations are at risk of exploitation.

Aboriginal rights and title

Prior to entering into treaty the Blackfoot Confederacy possessed a bundle of rights relating to water including proprietary interests in the rivers and riverbeds, rights to navigation, rights to gather aquatic plants and medicines, rights to hunt and rights to use water for a variety of domestic uses including drinking, washing, tanning hides, and watering stock. These practices, customs, and traditions involving water use were integral to the distinctive culture of the Blackfoot Confederacy and satisfy the test in *Sappier* to prove Aboriginal rights.

Effect of treaty 7 on water rights

The principles of treaty interpretation require common intention to establish the validity of terms of the treaty. There was no common intention of the parties to extinguish Aboriginal rights and title to water under Treaty 7. The black letter of the treaty includes a basket clause that purports to extinguish Aboriginal rights, but oral and written accounts of treaty negotiations reveal that the Chief had no intention of relinquishing their rights, titles, and interests to their waters.

Extinguishment of aboriginal and treaty rights by federal legislation and crown action

The North-west Irrigation Act, the only purpose of which was to replace riparian rights with a priority licencing system, did not clearly or plainly extinguish Aboriginal or treaty rights to water: Mere regulation does not extinguish Aboriginal rights. Neither did the NRTA extinguish Aboriginal and treaty rights. In fact, NRTA s.12 adds another layer of protection over treaty-protected Aboriginal rights, extends protection to the rights to fish and trap, and expands the area of protection to include the whole province. Arguably, the NRTA protects water rights which are incidental to the right to hunt, trap and fish. Any contemplated action that may negatively impact the right to hunt, trap, or fish anywhere in the province triggers the duty to consult with Treaty 7 First Nations.

The principles of constitutionalism and the rule of law mandate that provincial government action, including consultations with First Nations, must be consistent with the protection of existing Aboriginal and treaty rights. In so far as Alberta's consultation legislation, regulations, and policies have failed to fully recognize and affirm Aboriginal and treaty rights in a manner that is consistent with their constitutional protection, they are of no force or effect.

Consultation may take many forms ranging from mere notice to sharing information to consensus-building negotiations. The duty to consult has been interpreted by the Alberta government as being required only after lands have been designated for development and thereby "taken up" and before the project proponent receives approval for a particular project. Alberta views the duty to consult to arise on a project-by-project basis at each stage of development approval. This means that there is no comprehensive consultation for long-range sustainability of development, which is exactly what watershed management plans are about. Planning for sustainable development, including economic and community development requires shared governance of water resources. Alberta's Water for Life Strategy has failed in that regard, as it does not take into consideration the unique relationship of Treaty 7 First Nations to the Crown and treats Treaty 7 First Nations as any other "stakeholders" in the process of watershed planning.

If First Nations share in the governance of the watershed, they would be active participants in land use and water management planning for the watershed areas laying within their traditional territories. If their jurisdiction to manage the watershed was recognized, their consent may be required before approving any developments that may adversely effect the watershed.

This is not, however, how the current water management scheme works in Alberta. The province has not, to date, engaged First Nations in comprehensive watershed planning. Rather, Alberta has created policy directives that require project proponents to give notice to those who are "directly affected" by posting ads in local papers. After the proponent has created a proposal for development, the proponent must consider whether consultation with First Nations is required. If First Nations' traditional uses of the land may be adversely effected, consultation may be required, but the responsibility for consultation lays with the proponent. If First Nations were active participants in land water management planning there would be a standard set for considering all proposals – proposals might be rejected at the outset if they do not meet those standards.

The Alberta Water Council recognizes that there are difficulties with governing water use through multi-stakeholder volunteer Water Policy and Advisory Comittees. One of the major problems with WPACs is that First Nations do not participate in them. WPACs are organized by volunteers who do not engage First Nations because they do not fully understand the necessity of involving First Nations and, moreover, First Nation do not attend out of fear that their participation will be interpreted as consultation. First Nations feel that, as their relationship is with the Crown, they should be engaged in negotiations directly with the province and not with multi-stakeholders groups.

1. Questions for Further Research

This work is merely a beginning: There are very many more questions to be answered. Limited time and resources meant that I could not do any primary research. Much of the information that would have been useful in doing my research was privileged or buried in archives. To access this information would have required money and time resources that I did not have. I also did not have access to people who are well informed on the subject matter of my book. I have been slowly building a network of contacts with valuable experience in the area of Aboriginal water rights, some of whom have worked in the area their whole lives but have never written or published. I did not go to the archives, rather I relied heavily on historians such as

Frank Tough and Kinich Matsoui who have done the meticulous job of reviewing archival sources.

I attempted to access the points of view of Treaty 7 First Nations by contacting individuals responsible for land management at the various Band administration offices. However, I was contacted immediately by their counsel and warned not to talk to their clients – if I wanted any information I would have to go through counsel. As it turned out, counsel could not share information with me because water management in the process of negotiations and is privileged.

Members of the Alberta Water Council and the Bow River WPAC were also cautious in talking to me, but were willing to share some of the issues that they struggle with regarding consultation and shared governance. However, they could not offer many solutions to the problem without the involvement of First Nations.

The limitations and frustrations I encountered in finishing this book actually highlight the need and opportunity for further study.

Conclusions are supposed to be ends, but this conclusion is a beginning. Recently I attended a Legal Education Society of Alberta seminar on environmental law. There counsel to the EAB stated that the areas of environmental practice that are emerging as the most important and the least understood are consultation law and water law. That is certainly my experience in researching and writing this book. Every day I learn something new, but everything I have learned leads to more questions.

When I started writing this book, *Delgamu'ukw* was the leading consultation case and *Halfway River* had just been decided. *Taku* and *Haida* were decided shortly thereafter. Those who practiced Aboriginal law realized the establishment of the duty to consult was important First Nations, but no one dreamed how of what the impact would be. The duty to consult is now the platform on which First Nations resist such developments as the CANDU reactors near the Peace River, the Site C dam on the Peace River, and oilsands development along the Athabasca. The duty to consult will only become more important as we work through the practical meaning of "managing the Treaty relationship" and reconciling "aboriginal peoples and non-aboriginal peoples and their respective claims, interests and ambitions."[1]

---

[1] *Mikisew Cree First Nation* v. *Canada (Minister of Canadian Heritage)*, [2005] S.C.J. No. 71 (QL); 2005 SCC 69 at para 1.

Further research must be done on the legal history of water rights and water management for the various treaty areas. I devoted only one chapter to treaty rights to water, but legal historical research could be done to more fully analyze the existence and development of a treaty and Aboriginal rights to water.

Dovetailing with historical research should be a cultural linguistic study of Aboriginal laws relating to water. Because I speak and read only English, my research and writing was limited. There are many people in Treaty 7 who are fluent in their languages and could participate in a linguistic study of the meaning of the treaty, the practices, customs, and traditions involving water, and traditional relationships to water, governance, and treaty relationships. To determine the specific sites and how Aboriginal practices, customs, and traditions were conducted at those sites would require considerable research. In my view, the study of Aboriginal laws as they manifest in Aboriginal languages and cultures is the most important work to be done because law is in the language and in the land. The laws of Aboriginal people cannot be known without extensive inquiry into the workings of the language: Aboriginal laws are in embedded in Aboriginal languages, in their lexicon and organization. The only way to figure out how to reconcile the assertion of Crown sovereignty with pre-existing Aboriginal legal systems, is to study Aboriginal legal systems as articulated in their languages.

There is a great need for a handbook on best practices in Aboriginal consultation with industry and government. There is currently no national standard for consultation. Perhaps most importantly, further policy analysis must be done on the concept of reconciliation and the political process that best accomplish this gargantuan task. In my view, reconciliation will only truly be achieved when governance of water is shared with First Nations: The next phase political and legal evolution is to create a vision of shared governance of natural resources.

Further inquiry should be made into historical and cultural geography. As stated earlier, the law is in the land. The Blackfoot Confederacy described their territory as Napi's body. The territory addressed by Treaty 7 did not include the entire Blackfoot Confederacy territory. This raises interesting questions about whether there are different layers of Aboriginal and treaty rights inside and outside the treaty territory.

ADDENDUM: RECENT DEVELOPMENTS IN THE LAW IN ALBERTA

Recent jurisprudence coming out of the Alberta Court of Queen's Bench and Court of Appeal highlight the difficulties that First Nations encounter in Alberta in asserting their right to be consulted on matters affecting their rights to resources and to water in particular. My intention in commenting on recent case law is to shed light on moving forward in promoting the First Nations' rights to be consulted in Alberta.

In *Tsuu T'ina Nation et al. and the Samson Cree Nation et al.* v. *Alberta* [2] the Applicants requested a judicial review of the decisions of the Minister of Environment to approve the South Saskatchewan River Basin Plan and submit the Plan to Cabinet for approval. The *Water Act* and Water for Life Policy set out a process whereby watershed management plans can be created for each of the major watersheds. These watershed management plans, once complete, are submitted to the Minister of Environment for approval. Once approved by the Minister, the watershed management plans are the standard against which all future permits, licences, and allocations are to be vetted prior to approval. The First Nations claim that the Crown had failed to consult with them regarding their rights that may be adversely affected by the SSRB Management Plan, including the use and enjoyment of reserves, hunting and fishing rights, and Aboriginal water rights. Although the Plan reserved a portion of water rights for First Nations use, they argued that Crown had not discharged its duty to accommodate First Nations interests.

The Court of Queen's Bench ruled that there is no duty to consult at the planning stage of resource management. In coming to this conclusion, the Court appears to have dealt with the judicial review in a two-staged analysis: First, the Court characterized the Minister's approval of the Plan as a legislative act, assuming that this characterization eliminated the need to consider evidence of scope and nature of the right and impact on those rights. Second, having determined that the government act was legislative in nature, the Court decided to follow the *Sparrow* analysis by considering consultation at the justificatory stage of analysis.

Having completed the research for this book, it is my conclusion that the law of consultation has evolved over time, building on *Sparrow* and being developed by other landmark cases such as *Haida* and *Mikisew*. When a treaty governs the relationship between a First Nation and the Crown, that treaty relationship gives rise to a duty to consult on all contemplated

---

[2] *Tsuu T'ina Nation et al.* v. *Alberta*, 2008 ABQB 547, unreported at time of writing.

government action that may adversely affect the exercise of treaty rights such as livelihood rights and rights to a reserve.

In *Tsuu T'ina*, however, the Court took a very compartmentalized, static view of the duty to consult opposed to a more developmental and holistic view, and classified the duty into four distinct categories:

1. The right is proven and the government action is completed (as in *Sparrow*);
2. The right is proven and the government action is anticipated (as in *Mikisew*);
3. The right is claimed and the government action is anticipated (as in *Haida*); and
4. The right is claimed and the government action is completed (as in these Applications).[3]

Having decided that there was no proven Aboriginal or treaty right to water, and that the SSRB Management Plan had already been approved by the Minister and Cabinet, the Court used this classification system to decide that it was appropriate to distinguish the facts in *Mikisew* and *Haida* and apply only *Sparrow*. The Court was able to characterize the case as fitting into the fourth category despite the fact that counsel for the Tsuu T'ina and Samson Cree Nations, Clayton Leonard, submitted detailed historical evidence to establish the *prima facie* claim to a treaty right to water and evidence regarding the failure of the government to meaningfully consult with the First Nations leading up to the Plan.

Mr. Justice LoVecchio decided not to decide "whether the Applicants have a constitutionally protected "Aboriginal" or "Treaty" right to water either specifically or as an adjunct to other rights."[4] Herein lay the clay feet of this decision: The Court's failure to determine the nature and scope of the right claimed makes it impossible to adequately assess the impact on the rights claimed. Presumably, the Court thought that the Sparrow test does not require such an assessment, but on my reading of the law, this assumption is wrong.

Having characterized the situation as pertaining to unproven claims and completed government action, the Court turned to characterizing the government action as either administrative or legislative. There were two government "actions" subjected to judicial review:

> the decision of the Minister (Alberta Environment) to recommend the SSRB Plan to the Lieutenant Governor in Council for approval under the *Water Act*; and the decision of the Crown approving the SSRB Plan pursuant to section 11 of the *Water Act* which decision

---

[3] *Ibid.* at para 39.
[4] *Ibid.* at para 75.

was affirmed by Order in Council 409/2006, dated August 30, 2006.[5]

The Court concluded, relying on *Lefthand*, that Aboriginal consultation is not required prior legislative acts:

> It would be an unwarranted interference with the proper functioning of the House of Commons and the Provincial Legislatures to require that they engage in any particular processes prior to the passage of legislation. The same is true of the passage of regulations and Orders in Council by the appropriate Executive Council. <u>Enactments must stand or fall based on their compliance with the constitution, not based on the processes used to enact them.</u>[6] (emphasis mine)

In the Court's view, the relevant question is, therefore, whether the decisions of the Minister were administrative or legislative in nature. If approval of the watershed management plan is legislative in nature, then no duty to consult would arise. To answer that question, the Court relied on *Lefthand* and pointed out that:

> ...two characteristics are important in defining a legislative power. The first is the element of generality, that is, that the power is of general application and when exercised will not be directed at a particular person. The second indicium of a legislative power is that its exercise is based essentially on broad considerations of public policy, rather than on facts pertaining to individuals or their conduct.
>
> Decisions of a legislative nature, it is said, create norms or policy, whereas those of an administrative nature merely apply such norms to particular situations.[7]

Based on these considerations, the Court determined that the SSRB Plan is in fact a legislative act, regardless of the fact that it was created pursuant to the Water Act and the Water for Life Policy which defined the broader public policy relating to water governance:

> The SSRB Plan provides general considerations that must be taken into account by decision-makers exercising the authority given to them pursuant to the *Water Act*.
>
> It sets out the factors to be considered in whether to (I) issue an approval or licence or (ii) approve a transfer of an allocation of water in the area over which the water management plan applies [s. 11(3)(a) of the *Water Act*]. The *Water Act* specifically requires the Director to have regard to any plan in place when considering an application for a licence [s. 51(4)], when determining that licence applications should not be accepted in a water management area [s. 53(3)] and when considering an application for the transfer of a water allocation [s. 82(5)].
>
> When the subject matter of the SSRB Plan is considered, the action taken by the

---

[5] *Ibid.* at para 49.
[6] *R.* v. *Lefthand*, 2007 ABCA 206, [2007] A.W.L.D. 3264, [2007] A.W.L.D. 3317, [2007] A.W.L.D. 3265, [2007] A.W.L.D. 3318, [2007] A.W.L.D. 3263, [2007] A.W.L.D. 3267, [2007] A.W.L.D. 3266, [2007] A.W.L.D. 3316, [2007] 10 W.W.R. 1, 77 Alta. L.R. (4th) 203, 222 C.C.C. (3d) 129, [2007] 4 C.N.L.R. 281 at para 38.
[7] *Tsuu T'ina*, *supra* note 2 at para 62 and 63.

government is more legislative than administrative. As this legislative government action is completed, I agree with the Respondent, the Court is initially taken down the *Sparrow* fork in the road.[8]

Having determined that the SSRB Plan is a legislative act, LoVecchio J. felt he was left with only one choice:

> To the extent *Lefthand* has said there is no duty to consult for legislative acts, that decision is binding on me.[9]

Rather than taking the duty to consult as an evolutionary whole, he framed the situation in such a way that he distinguished it from the *Mikisew* and *Haida* decisions and that he was "bound" to follow the *Sparrow* analysis: Where a claimant is alleging that a completed government action is interfering with an established Aboriginal and treaty right, he must show that a *prima facie* infringement has occurred before the court will examine any other factors. Whether consultation has occurred is considered at the justificatory stage of the analysis. If the Court determines, as in this case, that no infringement has occurred, there is no need to assess whether the duty to consult has been met.

The *Lefthand* decision and its interpretation in *Tsuu T'ina* set precedent that puts Alberta's Aboriginal consultation law far behind that of other jurisdictions. First, *Tsuu T'ina* relieves the province from the responsibility of consulting with First Nations prior to setting provincial policy and passing legislation. If the definition of a legislative act is a Crown action which creates norms and policies to guide administrative decisions, then the approved provincial Consultation Guidelines fit that definition. As legislative acts, there is no duty to consult with First Nations prior to setting the Guidelines, despite the fact that they allow for annual review.

Second, *Tsuu T'ina* suggests that the only means for reviewing Alberta's consultation policy is a full-scale constitutional challenge. If First Nations are challenging government acts on the basis of failure to consult using a judicial review process, they must focus their challenge on procedural decisions of the government and not completed actions. That means that governments and industry proponents would only be held to the standard set by the provincial Constitutional Guidelines. If the Guidelines are challenged, they will be subject only to the *Sparrow* analysis, and not to a broader *Mikisew* analysis which would consider the larger questions of managing the treaty relationship.

---

[8] *Ibid.* at para 44.
[9] *Ibid.* at para 59.

In my view, for any future challenge of the Consultation Guidelines to be successful, it must be framed as a constitutional challenge. The applicant must do the work of proving that Alberta's Guidelines are inconsistent with s.35(1) protection of Aboriginal and treaty rights and are, therefore, of no force and effect under s.52 of the Constitution. (This argument has been suggested in chapter 2).

Third, *Tsuu T'ina* and *Lefthand* suggest that where there has been consultation over the broader issue of resource management, it is not necessary to have consultation with respect to each particular variation order, so long as the variation orders are within the general contemplation of the original consultation:

> There is also no duty to consult with respect to every minute decision made by government. If there has been adequate consultation with respect to a program or regime of regulation or development, that will satisfy the constitutional requirement for consultation. It is not thereafter necessary to consult again with respect to every administrative decision made to implement that strategy: *R. v. Douglas*, 2007 BCCA 265 (B.C. C.A.), at para. 42. That is so even if some particular decision arguably takes the program in a different direction or expands somewhat the parameters of the regime, so long as the new direction was fairly within the scope of the original consultation. Thus there was no fresh duty of consultation when the *Variation Orders* were renewed each year.[10]

Alberta's Consultation Guidelines could be interpreted as being "adequate consultation with respect to a program or regime or regulation or development." This raises some problems for First Nations who often feel like they are powerless by-standers observing the consumption of their traditional lands by government approved industrial development. For example, some First Nations would like to challenge the provincial Consultation Guidelines which only require consultation with impacted First Nations <u>after</u> leases are issued. For such a challenge to be effective, following the decisions of Alberta Courts, First Nations must challenge the constitutionality of the Guidelines – it is the only avenue open to them. The Guidelines set the consultation policy which is applied in the process of granting approvals. Provided that the proponent and the Minister follow the Guidelines, any argument regarding the failure of the proponent or the Crown to consult will be successfully defended by the fact that industry followed the Guidelines, regardless of the strength of the right.

Finally, in *Tsuu T'ina* the Court sidestepped dealing with First Nations jurisdiction over water by avoiding determining Aboriginal and treaty rights to water. Without a clear statement

---

[10] *Lefthand*, *supra* note 6 at para 40.

regarding First Nations jurisdiction in relation to water and unextinguished Aboriginal and treaty rights to water, the province will continue to govern water without sufficient consultation with First Nations. The up-side is that Aboriginal and treaty water rights, although undefined, are still protected by s.35(1) of the Constitution and First Nations may continue to assert these claims.

The question that will be asked by First Nations in Alberta is, "what do we do now?" Following *Tsuu T'ina*, Ministerial decisions that are quasi-legislative in nature can only be challenged on the basis of constitutionality. Thus, in order to move forward in the development of consultation law in Alberta, the next logical step is threefold: 1) Appeal *Tsuu T'ina;* 2) Challenge the constitutionality of the Alberta's Consultation Guidelines as a whole; and 3) Continue to assert jurisdiction to water and waterbeds within traditional territories.

BIBLIOGRAPHY

Statutes

Alberta Act, 4-5 Edward VII, c. 3 (Canada), [Assented to 20th July, 1905].

An Act respecting the Public Lands of the Dominion, 1872, Statutes of Canada, 35 Vict. 69, c.23.

The Constitution Act, 1867, 30 & 31 Victoria, c. 3. (U.K.)

Constitution Act, 1930, 20-21 George V, c. 26 (U.K.), Schedule 1.

Indian Act, R.S.C. 1985, c. I-5.

Irrigation Act, R.S.C. 1906, c.61

The North West Irrigation Act, S.C. 1894, c.30.

North-West Territories Act, R.S.C. 1886, c. 50.

The Royal Proclamation, October 7, 1763

Rupert's Land Act, 1868; 31-32 Victoria, c. 105 (U.K.)

Water Act, RSA 2000, c. W-3.

Treaties and Agreements

Treaty No. 7, made 22nd Sept., 1877, between her Majesty the Queen and the Blackfeet and other Indian Tribes, at the Blackfoot Crossing of the Bow River, Fort Macleod (Ottawa: Queen's Printer and controller of Stationery, 1966).

Peigan Agreement.

Case Law

Apsassin et al. v. *B.C. Oil and Gas Commission et al.* (2004), 2004 BCCA 286, 8 C.E.L.R. (3d) 161, 201 B.C.A.C. 78, [2004] 4 C.N.L.R. 340, 2004 CarswellBC 1276.

Attorney-General of Canada v. *Aluminum Company of Canada Limited and Attorney-General of British Columbia*, [1987] 1 C.N.L.R. 10.

Barthel v. *Scotten* (1895), 24 Can. S.C.R. 367.

Blueberry River Indian Band v. *Canada (Department of Indian Affairs and Northern Development)*, [1995] 4 S.C.R. 344.

Brand v. *Griffin* (1908) 1 Alta. L. R. 510.

Calder v. *British Columbia (Attorney-General)*, [1973] S.C.R. 313.

Canadian Pacific Ltd. v. *Paul*, [1988] 2 S.C.R. 654.

Claxton v. *Saanichton Marina Ltd.*, [1989] 3 C.N.L.R. 46.

Delgamu'ukw v. *British Columbia*, [1997] S.C.J. No. 108 (QL); [1997] 3 S.C.R. 1010.

Derrickson v. *Derrickson*, [1986] 2 C.N.L.R. 45.

Edwards v. *Attorney-General for Canada*, [1930] A.C. 124 (P.C.), at p. 136.

Flewelling v. *Johnston* (1921), 59 D.L.R. 419 (Alta. S.C., A.D.), [1921] 2 W.W.R. 374.

Frank v. *The Queen*, [1978] 1 S.C.R. 95.

Friends of the Oldman River Society v. *Canada (Minister of Transport)* [1992] 1 S.C.R. 3.

Fort George Lumber Co. v. *Grand Trunk Pacific R. Co.*, (1915), 24 D.L.R. 527.

Guerin v. *Canada*, [1984] S.C.J. No. 45; [1984] 2 S.C.R. 335; 13 D.L.R. (4th) 321.

Haida Nation v. *British Columbia (Minister of Forests)*, [2004] 3 S.C.R. 511; [2004] S.C.J. No. 70 (Q.L.); 2004 SCC 73.

Halfway River First Nation v. *British Columbia (Ministry of Forests)*, [1997] 4 C.N.L.R. 45.

Halfway River First Nation v. *British Columbia (Ministry of Forests)*, [1999] 4 C.N.L.R. 1 (B.C.C.A.) at 44

Hamlet of Baker Lake et al. v. *Minister of Indian Affairs and Northern Development et al.*, [1979] 3 C.N.L.R. 17.

Heiltsuk Tribal Council v. *British Columbia (Minister of Sustainable Resource Management)* (2003), 19 B.C.L.R. (4th) 107 (B.C.S.C.).

Jack v. *The Queen*, [1980] 1 S.C.R. 294.

Johnston v. *O'Neill*, [1911] A.C. 552 (H.L.).

Jules v. *Harper Ranch Ltd.*, [1991] 1 C.N.L.R. 76.

Keewatin Power Co. v. *Kenora (Town)* (1906), 13 O.L.R. 237 (H.C.).

Lac La Ronge Indian Band v. *Canada,* 2002 CarswellSask 626; [2002] 4 C.N.L.R. iv (note); 302 N.R. 197 (note); 241 Sask. R. 78 (note); 313 W.A.C. 78 (note).

Mathias Colomb Band of Indians v. *Saskatchewan Power Corp.*, [1994] 4 C.N.L.R. 50.

Mikisew Cree First Nation v. *Canada (Minister of Canadian Heritage),* [2005] S.C.J. No. 71 (QL); 2005 SCC 69.

Moosehunter v. *The Queen,* [1981] 1 S.C.R. 282.

Okanagan Indian Band v. *Deputy Comptroller of Water Rights,* [1999] 3 C.N.L.R. 190.

Osoyoos Indian Band v. *Oliver (Town),* [2001] S.C.J. No. 82; 2001 SCC 85; [2001] 3 S.C.R. 746.

Pasco v. *Canadian National Railway Co.,* [1986] 1 C.N.L.R. 34.

Paul et al. v. *Canadian Pacific Ltd. et al.,* 2 D.L.R. (4th) 22.

Re British Columbia Fisheries, (1913), 11 D.L.R. 255 at 263, aff'd (1913), 15 D.L.R. 308 (P.C.).

Reference re Secession of Quebec, [1998] S.C.J. No. 61 (QL); [1998] 2 S.C.R. 217.

Reference re Same-Sex Marriage, [2004] S.C.J. No. 75 (QL); 2004 SCC 79; [2004] 3 S.C.R. 698.

Re Iverson and Greater Winnipeg Water District, (1921), 57 D.L.R. 184.

Re Provincial Fisheries (1896), 26 Can. S.C.R. 444.

R. v. *Adams,* [1996] 3 S.C.R. 101; 138 D.L.R. (4th) 657; 202 N.R. 89; 110 C.C.C. (3d) 97; [1996] 4 C.N.L.R. 1.

R. v. *Big M Drug Mart Ltd.,* [1985] S.C.J. No. 17; [1985] 1 S.C.R. 295.

R. v. *Blais,* [2003] 2 S.C.R. 236; [2003] S.C.J. No. 44; 2003 SCC 44.

R. v. *Badger,* [1996] 1 S.C.R. 771; [1996] S.C.J. No. 39 (QL).

R. v. *Bernard,* [2003] 4 C.N.L.R. 48, rev'g *R.* v. *Bernard,* [2002] 3 C.N.L.R. 114, appealed to the Supreme Court, [2005] 3 C.N.L.R. 214.

R. v. *Coté,* [1996] S.C.J. No. 93; [1996] 3 S.C.R. 139; 138 D.L.R. (4th) 385; 202 N.R. 161; [1996] 4 C.N.L.R. 26.

R. v. *Dick,* [1985] 2 S.C.R. 309; [1985] S.C.J. No. 62 (QL).

R. v. *Gladstone,* [1996] 2 S.C.R. 723; [1996] S.C.J. No. 79 (QL).

R. v. *Horseman*, [1990] S.C.J. No. 39 (QL); [1990] 1 S.C.R. 901.

R. v. *Lefthand*, 2007 ABCA 206, [2007] A.W.L.D. 3264, [2007] A.W.L.D. 3317, [2007] A.W.L.D. 3265, [2007] A.W.L.D. 3318, [2007] A.W.L.D. 3263, [2007] A.W.L.D. 3267, [2007] A.W.L.D. 3266, [2007] A.W.L.D. 3316, [2007] 10 W.W.R. 1, 77 Alta. L.R. (4th) 203, 222 C.C.C. (3d) 129, [2007] 4 C.N.L.R. 281.

R. v. *Lewis*, [1996] 1 S.C.R. 921; [1996] S.C.J. No. 46 (QL).

R. v. *Marshall*, [1999] 4 C.N.L.R. 161; [1999] 3 S.C.R. 456; [1999] S.C.J. No. 55 (QL).

R. v. *Marshall* (II), [1999] 4 C.N.L.R. 301.

R. v. *Marshall*; R. v. *Bernard*, [2005] S.C.J. No. 44; 2005 SCC 43; [2005] 2 S.C.R. 220; 255 D.L.R. (4th) 1; [2005] 3 C.N.L.R. 214; 2005 CarswellNS 317.

R. v. *Morgentaler*, [1993] S.C.J. No. 95; [1993] 3 S.C.R. 463.

R. v. *Nikal*, [1996] 1 S.C.R. 1013; [1996] S.C.J. No. 47 (QL).

R. v. *Noel*, [1995] 4 C.N.L.R. 78.

R. v. *Nowegijick*, [1983] 1 S.C.R. 29.

R. v. *N.T.C. Smokehouse Ltd.*, [1996] 2 S.C.R. 672.

R. v. *Sikyea* (1964), 43 D.L.R. (2d) 150 at 152 (N.W.T.C.A.); aff'd [1964] S.C.R. 642.

R. v. *Simon*, [1985] 2 S.C.R. 387; [1985] S.C.J. No. 67.

R. v. *Sioui*; 1990 CarswellQue 103; [1990] 1 S.C.R. 1025, 109 N.R. 22, 56 C.C.C. (3d) 225, 70 D.L.R. (4th) 427, [1990] 3 C.N.L.R. 127.

R. v. *Sparrow*, [1990] 1 S.C.R. 1075; [1990] S.C.J. No. 49.

R. v. *Sundown*, [1999] 1 S.C.R. 393; [1999] S.C.J. No.13 (QL).

R. v. *Sutherland*, [1980] 2 S.C.R. 451.

R. v. *Van der Peet*, [1996] S.C.J. No. 77, [1996] 2 S.C.R. 507.

Rex v. *Cyr* (1917), 38 D.L.R. 601, 29 Can. Cr. Cas. 77, 12 Alta L.R. 320.

Roberts v. *Canada*, [1989] 1 S.C.R. 322.

Sawridge Band v. *Canada*, [1995] 4 C.N.L.R. 121 at 143.

St. Mary's Indian Band v. *Cranbrook (City)*, [1997] 2 S.C.R. 657, aff'g [1996] 2 C.N.L.R. 222.

Taku River Tlingit First Nation v. *British Columbia (Project Assessment Director)*, [2004] 3 S.C.R. 550; [2004] S.C.J. No. 69; 2004 SCC 74.

Tsuu T'ina Nation et al. v. *Alberta*, 2008 ABQB 547

Wewaykum Indian Band v. *Canada*, [2002] 4 S.C.R. 245; [2002] S.C.J. No. 79 (QL); 2002 SCC 79.

Winters v. *United States*, 207 U.S. 564 (1908), 52 L.Ed. 340 aff'g 143 F.740 (9th Cir. 1906)

Secondary Sources

Alberta Environment, "First Nation Consultation Guidelines (Regulatory Authorizations and Environmental Impact Assessments) Draft 1, May 18, 2006" accessed at http://www.aand.gov.ab.ca/AANDFlash/Files/AENV_FN_Guidelines_Draft_1_May_18_2006.pdf, on July 31, 2006.

Nigel Bankes, "Delgamu'ukw, Division of Powers and Provincial Land and Resource Laws: Some Implications for Provincial Resource Rights" (1998) 32 U. Brit. Colum. L. Rev. 317.

N. Bankes, "Indian Resource Rights and Constitutional Enactments in Western Canada, 1871-1930" in L. Knafla, ed. *Law and Justice in a New Land: Essays in Western Canadian Legal History*, (Calgary: Carswell, 1986) at 129-164.

Nigel Bankes and L. Douglas Rae, "Recent Cases on the Calculation of Royalties on First Nations' Lands" (2000) 38 Alta. L. Rev. 258.

Richard H. Bartlett, *Aboriginal Water Rights in Canada: A Study of Aboriginal Title to Water and Indian Water Rights*, (Calgary: Canadian Institute of Resources Law, 1988).

Richard Bartlett, "Indian Reserves on the Prairies" (1985) 23 Alta. L. Rev. 243.

Rose Boyko Wuerscher, "Title to the Water Bed: The Legal History of the Ad Medium Filum Aqaue Rule" (1982) Department of Indian and Northern Affairs Canada, unpublished.

John Borrows, *Recovering Canada: The Resurgence of Indigenous Law*, (Toronto: University of Toronto Press, 2002).

John Borrows, "Tracking Trajectories: Aboriginal Governance as an Aboriginal Right" (2005) 38 U.B.C. L. Rev. 285.

Peggy Brizinski, *Knots in a String: An Introduction to Native Studies in Canada*, (Saskatoon: University Extension Press, University of Saskatchewan, 1993)

Canadian Council of Ministers of the Environment, "Guidelines for Consultations and Partnerships: Involving Stakeholders in CCME" undated, access at http://www.ccme.ca/assets/pdf/gdlns_consultns_partnshps_stkhldrs_e.pdf on July 31, 2006.

Gordon Christie, "Delgamu'ukw and the Protection of Aboriginal Land Interests," 32 Ottawa L. Rev. 85 2000-2001.

Michael Coyle, "Loyalty and Distinctiveness: A New Approach to the Crown's Fiduciary Duty Toward Aboriginal Peoples" (2003) 40 Alta. L. Rev.841.

Gordon Christie, "Justifying Principles of Treaty Interpretation" (2000) 26 Queen's L. J. 143.

Gordon Christie, "*Delgamu'ukw* and the Protection of Aboriginal Land Interests" (2000-2001) 32 Ottawa L. Rev. 85.

Hugh Dempsey, *Crowfoot: Chief of the Blackfeet* (Halifax: Goodread Biographies, 1988).

Hugh Dempsey, *Red Crow: Warrior Chief* (Saskatoon: Fifth House, Ltd., 1995).

Timothy Dickson, "Self-Government by Side Agreement?" (2004) 49 McGill L.J. 419.

P. S. Elder, "Environmental Impact Assessment in Canada: The Slave River Project" (1986) 24 Alta. L. Rev. 205.

David E. Elliott, "Much Ado About Dittos: Wewaykum and the Fiduciary Obligation of the Crown" (2003) 29 Queen's L.J. 1.

Daniel Francis, Toby Morantz, *Partners in Furs: A History of the Fur Trade in Eastern James Bay, 1600-1870*, (McGill-Queen's University Press: 2003).

André Goldenberg, "Salmon for Peanut Butter: Equality, Reconciliation and the Rejection of Commercial Aboriginal Rights" (2004) 3 Indigenous L. J. 61.

Mary Griffiths and Dan Woynillowicz, *Oil and Troubled Waters: Reducing the impact of the oil and gas industry on Alberta's water resources*. (Pembina Institute)

James (Sákéj) Youngblood Henderson, "Interpreting Sui Generis Treaties" (1997) 36 Alta. L. Rev. 47.

James (Sákéj) Youngblood Henderson, "Postcolonial Indigenous Legal Consciousness" (2002) 1 Indigenous L.J. 1.

James [Sákéj] Youngblood Henderson, "Empowering Treaty Federalism" (1994) Saskatchewan Law Review 158.

Michael Hudson, "Reconciling Diversity with Unity: Canadian Federalism in the 21st Century" unpublished paper presented to the Canadian Bar Association Canadian Legal Conference in Vancouver, August 14-16, 2005.

Shin Imai, "Treaty Lands and Crown Obligations: The 'Tracts Taken Up' Provision" (2001) 27 Queen's L. J. 1.

Shin Imai, "Sound Science, Careful Policy Analysis, and Ongoing Relationships: Integrating Litigation and Negotiation in Aboriginal Lands and Resources Disputes" (2003) 41 Osgoode Hall L. J. 587.

Indian Claims Commission, Annual Report 1997-1998, Minister of Public Works and Government Services Canada, 1998.

Thomas Isaac and Anthony Knox, "Canadian Aboriginal Law: Creating Certainty in Resource Development" (2004) 53 U.N.B.L.J. 3.

Thomas Isaac and Anthony Knox, "The Crown's Duty to Consult Aboriginal People" (2003) 41 Alta. L. Rev. 49.

G. V. La Forest, *Water law in Canada: The Atlantic Provinces*, Dept. of Regional Economic Expansion (1973).

S. Lawrence and P. Macklem, "From Consultation to Reconciliation: Aboriginal Rights and the Crown's Duty to Consult" (2000), 79 *Can. Bar Rev.* 252.

Alistair R. Lucas, "Canadian Participatory Rights in Energy Resource Development: The Bridges to Empowerment?" (2004) 24 J. Land Resources & Envtl. L. 195.

Leonard Mandamin, "Water Rights on Alberta Indian Reserves" (1980) unpublished.

Louise Mandel, "Jurisdiction over Water on Indian Reserves under Treaty 7 in Alberta" obtained from Ron Maurice.

David G. Mandelbaum, *The Plains Cree* (New York : AMS Press, 1979).

Kinichi Matsui, *Reclaiming Indian Waters: Dams, Irrigation, and Indian Water Rights in Western Canada: 1858-1930*, PhD. Thesis (Vancouver: U.B.C., 2003) at 32-33.

Theresa A. McClenaghan, "Why Should Aboriginal Peoples Exercise Governance Over Environmental Issues?" (2002) 51 U.N.B.L.J. 211.

Kent McNeil, "The Meaning of Aboriginal Title," In Michael Asch, ed. *Aboriginal and Treaty Rights in Canada*. (Vancouver: U.B.C. Press, 1997) 135.

Kent McNeil, "Aboriginal Title and Aboriginal Rights: What's the Connection?" (1997) 36 Alta. L. Rev. 117.

Kent McNeil, "Aboriginal Title and the Division of Powers: Rethinking Federal and Provincial Jurisdiction" (1998) 61 Sask. L. Rev. 431.

Kent McNeil, *Common Law Aboriginal Title* (Oxford: Clarendon Press, 1989).

Alexander Morris, *The Treaties of Canada with the Indians of Manitoba and the North-West Territories including the Negotiations on which they were based* (Toronto: Belfords, Clarke & Co., 1880).

F. David Peat, *Lighting the Seventh Fire: The Spiritual Ways, Healing, and Science of the Native American* (Secaucus, N.J.: Carol Publishing Group, 1994).

David Percy, "Seventy-Five Years of Alberta Water Law: Maturity, Demise & Rebirth" (1996) 35 Alta. L. Rev. 221.

David Percy, "Water Rights in Alberta" (1977) 15 Alta. L. Rev. 142.

Mark Rappaport, "Bringing Meaning to first Nations Consultation in the British Columbia Salmon Aquaculture Industry" (2005) 14 Dalhousie J. Legal Stud. 146.

Monique M. Ross and Cheryl Y. Sharvit, "Forest Management in Alberta and Rights to Hunt, Trap and Fish Under Treaty 8" (1998) 36 Alta. L. Rev. 645.

Leonard I. Rotman, "Wewaykum: A New Spin on the Crown's Fiduciary Obligations to Aboriginal Peoples?" (2004) 37 U.B.C. L. Rev. 219.

J. Saunders, *Interjurisdictional Issues in Canadian Water Management* (Calgary: Canadian Institute of Resources Law, 1988) at 89-91.

Graham R. Statt, "Tapping into Water Rights: An Exploration of Native Entitlement in the Treaty 8 Area of Northern Alberta" (2003) 18 Can. J. L. & Soc. 103.

Brian Slattery, Making Sense of Aboriginal and Treaty Rights" [2000] 79 Can. Bar Rev. 196.

Frank J. Tough, "The Forgotten Constitution: The Natural Resources Transfer Agreements and Indian Livelihood Rights, CA. 1925-1933" 2004 41 Alta. L. Rev. 999.

Frank J. Tough, "Treaty Rights to a Livelihood" (Winnipeg: Public Interest Law Centre,1998), unpublished.

Treaty 7 Elders and Tribal Council with Walter Hildebrandt, Sarah Carter, and Dorothy First Rider, The True Spirit and Original Intent of Treaty 7 (Montreal: McGill-Queen's University Press, 1996).

Kenneth J. Tyler, "The Division of Powers and Aboriginal Water Rights Issues": National Symposium on Water Law, Environmental Law CLE Programme, 1999, unpublished.

Wissenschaftlicher Buchverlag bietet

kostenfreie

Publikation

von

wissenschaftlichen Arbeiten

Diplomarbeiten, Magisterarbeiten, Master und Bachelor Theses
sowie Dissertationen, Habilitationen und wissenschaftliche Monographien

Sie verfügen über eine wissenschaftliche Abschlußarbeit zu aktuellen oder zeitlosen Fragestellungen, die hohen inhaltlichen und formalen Ansprüchen genügt, und haben **Interesse an einer honorarvergüteten Publikation**?

Dann senden Sie bitte erste Informationen über Ihre Arbeit per Email an info@vdm-verlag.de. Unser Außenlektorat meldet sich umgehend bei Ihnen.

VDM Verlag Dr. Müller Aktiengesellschaft & Co. KG
Dudweiler Landstraße 125a
D - 66123 Saarbrücken

www.vdm-verlag.de